Approaching a Pedagogy of Game Writing

This book examines the practices of writers in the AAA video game industry, to provide a model for game writing pedagogy that highlights the roles and skills utilized by these innovative storytellers.

Based on a two-year qualitative study, gathering data through conversational interviews, Seth Hudson combines theory, practice, and his experience as an educator-researcher to shed light on the phenomenon of game writing and writers who drive innovation in game storytelling. The author gives context for a range of audiences, examining the role of computer game design (CGD) in higher education, the role of writing and narrative design within those programs, the current and historical challenges game writers face, and the purpose of the research underpinning this book. Hudson frames a synthesis of research findings and relevant theory to illustrate new teaching practices informed by his findings that will help better serve students.

This book will provide an essential resource for game studies and game design educators and researchers, as well as game narrative enthusiasts.

Seth Hudson is Associate Professor of Game Writing in the Computer Game Design program at George Mason University, where he teaches Story Design for Computer Games, Criticism and Research Methods, and the History of Computer Games. Hudson's scholarship explores playful approaches to teaching; game writing pedagogy; portfolio-focused curriculum development; and undergraduate student research and creative activity.

Approaching a Pedagogy of Game Writing

Seth Hudson

Routledge
Taylor & Francis Group

NEW YORK AND LONDON

First published 2023
by Routledge
605 Third Avenue, New York, NY 10158

and by Routledge
4 Park Square, Milton Park, Abingdon, Oxon, OX14 4RN

Routledge is an imprint of the Taylor & Francis Group, an informa business

Library of Congress Cataloging-in-Publication Data
A catalog record for this title has been requested

ISBN: 978-1-032-23145-7 (hbk)
ISBN: 978-1-032-23450-2 (pbk)
ISBN: 978-1-003-27766-8 (ebk)

DOI: 10.4324/9781003277668

Typeset in Times New Roman
by codeMantra

This book is dedicated to the video game writing community who continue to push the medium forward with their creativity, empathy, and love of the craft.

Contents

1 CGD in Higher Education, Briefly   1
Background: CGD as Field of Study 2
Disparate Disciplines 4
Industry Perceptions 6
The Way Forward 7

2 Game Writing in Contexts   9
Industry Context 9
CGD/Higher Education Context 16
Educator-Researcher Context 20
Designing the Study 26
Data Collection 28
Reflection: So What? (… and for Whom?) 31

3 Approaching Game Writing/Writers   36
Purpose 36
Participant Overview 38
Three Essential Roles of the Game Writer 39
Five Areas of Competence/Functional Competencies 39
"This Doesn't Have Anything to Do with Game
   Design."—Margaret 40
"The Ability to Say, 'Yeah, All Right.'"—Micah 46
"It's About Finding Balance."—Lou 51
"It's All Different Thinking"—Peter 57
"You're the Wrapper."—Garreth 62
"How Long Is a Piece of String?"—Henry 69
"Logic Matters. Doing Math Matters."—Robert 75
'Summary of Results 82

4   Developing a Pedagogy of Game Writing   85
From the Lobby to the Classroom and Back Again 85
CGD: "What to teach?" vs. "How to teach it?" 86
Those Who Can Teach... 87
Bridging Education and Industry through Scholarship 88
Fusing the Languages of Industry and Education 89

5   Areas of Competence, Essential Roles   91
Essential Roles 91
Areas of Competence for Game Writers 92

6   Deploying a Pedagogy of Game Writing   96
Implementation in the Classroom 96
Experimentation in the Classroom 104
Identifying Relevant Coursework 104
Inclusion across CGD Coursework 105
Specialty-Specific Portfolios 105
Conclusion 106

Epilogue   107
Now It's Your Turn 108
Doing the Work vs. Getting Paid to Do the Work 109
Finding Fulfillment 110

Index   113

1 CGD in Higher Education, Briefly

Writing as an educator-researcher in the field, it is easy to take the context of computer game design (CGD) for granted. This chapter offers some background on CGD as a field of study, including some of the unique challenges that face these programs, their faculty, and students.

I should introduce myself before we get started. My pursuit of knowing an ill-defined field was borne out of my desire to be a better educator. Leaving the station around 2011, my first stop was the library. I reviewed the available literature on game writing, mostly trade press books, and didn't find the kind of depth necessary—at least in my stodgy, academic view—for pedagogical development. The best practices on teaching that are part of my core beliefs and pillars of practice did not seem to translate.

The industry-borne texts were a curiosity-satisfying pleasure to read, except for those that felt thousands of words giving watery overviews of outdated storytelling concepts necessary but didn't have the theoretical grounding in Writing Studies or Education required for my purpose. I'll reference several of these texts as we go. You really should check them out to learn from the expertise of those authors and/or gain fresh perspectives on game writing; if you're too busy to read all of them, though, I'll sum it up like this: "Writing for games is unlike anything else."

Were this true in an absolute sense, game writing should be easy to identify, right? Not so fast. Rather than expertise blindness, it was time for me to don my expertise goggles(?). In Writing Studies, defining rhetorical genre—a phenomenon I'll address in some depth later on—first requires the examination of texts that represent the work done to create that product. Unfortunately,

(Continued)

DOI: 10.4324/9781003277668-1

there is no set format for game writers and the tools are customized to a particular project within a particular studio. So much for that first step in defining the genre.

I am an educator and a researcher, curious to a fault and convinced that there's usually more for me and my students to know, and almost always a better way to teach it.

Background: CGD as Field of Study

CGD programs in higher education have existed and flourished for over 25 years, with growing student enrollments and top-tier faculty increasing recognized across the academy for the creative and scholarly achievements. Walking the line between industry preparedness and a well-rounded, creativity-fostering, intellectually stimulating curriculum that many disciplines face in higher education today, CGD programs must also deal with popular perceptions of the medium. Some may the pursuit of video games in an educational setting as a frivolous pursuit.

Many institutions offer course work in computer programming and digital arts; the layperson may see these as sufficient for students seeking a career in games. After all, the individuals who built the billion-dollar industry we know today had no formal training in game design. This complicates the notion that CGD programs emerged to meet the industry's increasing demand for skilled labor (Davidson, 2010).

The range of student perceptions further complicates matters. The first viewpoint is that of the games-enthusiast student—as a heads up to the reader, my belief in this assumption runs throughout the book—whose affinity for the medium is central to their decision to pursue CGD. In extreme cases, these game-enthusiast students enroll with visions of playing games for academic credit. These games-enthusiast students, and whoever funds their education, may adhere to the belief that their degree will result in a specific job post-postgraduation, that their choice of academic degree is ultimately their choice of profession. Increasingly, this is not the usual case. A degree has intrinsic value and correlates with higher lifetime earnings, but it is rarely a straight line from program to industry. The game industry continues to place more value on applicants' portfolio of work rather than attainment of a particular degree (Brathwaite & Schreiber, 2011). The games-enthusiast student who fails to embrace this reality may be in for a rude awakening.

A second perspective comes from a more industrious student who enters the course of study understanding the portfolio's primacy, one who has the focus and will to build whatever skills are necessary to find employment post-graduation; let's call them the games-as-career student. This student has a sense of "portfolio always wins," and has already undertaken self-training in many of the industry-grade tools—Blender, Unity, RPG Maker, etc.—available at little to no cost, spending as much time watching tutorials and making their own projects as they do playing games or watching streamers.

The games-as-career student may be driven by visions of creating the next crowdfunded indie hit, or they may be imbued with the game design community's ethos of self-training (Ashton, 2010; Newman, 2013). Another, much simpler explanation: these students may just be intelligent and hard working. If you're an educator—regardless of your discipline—you already know that clever, curious, hard-working students are the most likely to be successful.

> In a previous administrative role, one of my jobs was to oversee recruitment of potential students. Sandra made an appointment to learn more about the program; she started the discussion by saying, "I already have a degree. I don't necessarily plan on graduating here, I just want to learn enough to get in the industry." After a few years building a portfolio, Sandra found an internship at an AAA company. It went well. She never returned (and has made quite a career in the years since). Whenever students worry that a job opportunity, usually an internship, will delay their graduation, I tell them: "Take the job. Hopefully we'll still be here if you want to come back; this professional opportunity may never come again."

CDG programs' particular curricular needs are not wholly unique. Offering students enhanced access to internship; supporting original undergraduate research, creative activity, and scholarship; and incorporating both oral and written communication across the curriculum are staples at many institutions. Notable for CGD is the absolute need for these as students' ticket in the industry will come through the work they create (and can show) rather than the degree they possess.

Post-graduation, successful job applicants must show work that demonstrates the competencies required of a position. In the highly collaborative practice of game development, demonstrating individual

Table 1.1 CGD Course Availability Sample (HEVGA, 2015)

Course	Required of All Students (%)	Required in Some Specializations (%)	Elective (%)	Not Available (%)
Interactive narrative	24.2	19.7	21.2	30.3
Animation	22.7	31.8	21.2	21.2
Game research	24.2	13.6	31.8	24.2
Game programming	31.8	24.2	25.8	16.7
Critical game studies	30.3	4.5	21.2	39.4
Project courses	56.1	6.1	12.1	19.7

contributions can be difficult. This lack of explicit authorship presents a unique challenge for CDG students. Programs should make collaborative student production a priority, while also helping students to highlight their contributions or to create some individually authored work for a portfolio.

Beyond presenting demonstrable skills in the technical components of game development, students face the further challenge of demonstrating the higher-order thinking skills that make them more appealing to potential employers. Combining reflections on their contributions and the process of collaboration is one way for students to demonstrate a capacity for self-critique and critical thinking.

The ideal programs would be those that challenge students with opportunities to work hard and explore. While the majority of programs do require some kind of "project course" (see Table 1.1), the value of student production may be lost if not contextualized. Reflecting on the process of collaboration, considering the influences and implications of design choices, situating work in relationship to society and culture: these are the things that make the "project course" truly valuable.

Devoid of context, students in these courses just make stuff. Our assumption is that their skills develop to some degree in the process. Providing a CGD education that incorporates context allows us to develop students, at a minimum, as makers of stuff. We can stress reflection on the design/production process, on personal growth, and help ensure that students leave with more than a collection of "stuff" they worked on.

Disparate Disciplines

In the face of the questions regarding the value of a degree in CGD, programs have the opportunity to reshape thinking about higher education and the student experience. Making games requires a complex combination of art and technology. The academic disciplines associated with the elements of a game are not so easily combined, perhaps; those with experience in higher education know that creating an academic degree program requires more than making a list of courses.

Satisfying university requirements for assessment is just one step in a process. Programs must meet the expectations of external, discipline-specific accreditation bodies in addition to any requirements of their particular region or state. Though they may share the outcome of preparing students for the game industry, a degree housed in a school of art will necessarily look different than one housed in a school of engineering—not to mention issues in scheduling and resource allocation that pose challenges for cross-disciplinary programs.

The Higher Education Video Game Association (HEVGA) published their first survey of CGD programs in 2015, as *Our State of Play (2015)*. Regarding curriculum, the kinds of courses offered from various disciplines were fairly scattered. The report touted this disparity as evincing the breadth and dynamism of the field; that may well be true, but such chaos brings complications for instructors, researchers, institutions, and, most importantly, students aspiring to the game industry.

Rather than deciding on which CGD program best suits their needs, students must first identify what any given program actually is. Interactive narrative, for example, is required coursework for 24.2% of the programs in the HEVGA (2015) survey, but it is not available at 30.3% of schools. The same goes for other areas of study: animation—required of 24.2%, not available at 21.2%; game programming—required of 31.8%, not available at 16.7%; and critical game studies—required of 30.3%, not available at 39.4%. In fact, only "project courses" are required by a majority of CGD programs, just barely, at 56.1%. Keep in mind, they're not available at 19.7%.

The range of disciplines mirrors perceptions of game development. What is the most important element in a game? With such a range of requirements for sound, story, art, design—not to mention all the management necessary to keep a team of hundreds moving forward—it is difficult to know where to place focus. Should the games-as-career student become a master of just one element, or would they benefit from a generalist approach where they engage in all the facets of game development?

Some students considering CGD programs may be drawn by the 121,459 USD in compensation on average, as reported by the Entertainment Software Association (Tripp et al., 2019), earned by AAA industry employees. The value of such a degree is questionable, however, as a degree is not always required to work in the industry (Brathwaite & Schreiber, 2011; Dille & Platten, 2008). In the industry, some professionals question if game design can be taught at all (Ashton, 2010). Some academics, however, assert that instruction adequate to prepare students for the industry is beyond the scope of a four-year-degree program. In the words of James Portnow (Extra Credits, 2012), an industry veteran, frequent contributor to the *Extra Credits* web series, and faculty member at DigiPen Institute of Technology, students have "more to learn about games than [CGD programs] can ever teach you."

Over the last 20 or so years, a critical mass of scholars and educators have begun to conceptualize a new academic field focused on the aesthetics, technologies, and cultures of video games, unhindered by the conventions of traditional disciplines (Aarseth, 2002). This Game Studies movement is surely part of the many CGD programs still surfacing, but a field that is unhindered—unbothered, really—by traditional disciplines is a hard sell.

From my point of view as an educator, the generalist approach seems most promising as it will prepare students for success in any number of pursuits after graduation. Presenting students with opportunities to explore their chosen field or discipline is vital to a well-rounded education. Employers may not agree. With a need for XYZ tasks to be completed in production, their preference may be an individual who can do one thing very well. You don't need to understand the whole assembly line, you just need to stay at your station and get the job done.

Industry Perceptions

While the efforts to assist CGD are well-meaning, industry attempts to do so often fail to take educational realities into account. While industry practitioners—not just in games, certainly—have many opinions regarding what we should be teaching students, the "portfolio always wins" sentiment seems to ring true. A portfolio allows prospective employees to demonstrate skills in specific tools. "Show, don't tell" applies, here. One's résumé can include an impressive list of software or even reference small indie projects they've completed, but with no way to actually see or play the work, those lists of software and names and titles are just words on a page.

For professional writers of all types, generally, the writing portfolio is nothing new. Writers collate and curate their best work to demonstrate their skills. Rather than mere technical proficiency in using a particular software tool—basic composition and editing are an assumed requisite for writers—these portfolios represent a process and personal approach to creation. Reviewing writing samples is a search for the author. The use of voice, pacing, evocative vocabulary; variation in genres, literary and thematic; and awareness of audience and tone should not be difficult to find if the writer has constructed their portfolio thoughtfully and tailored it to the situation.

For game writers and those looking to hire them, the portfolio is something different, something a bit more nuanced. Aspiring game writers able to show interactive work have an edge but must not overlook the fundamentals of storytelling. The ability to work with technological bells and whistles is requisite for certain subdisciplines of game design, but their importance is far less in writing. What's more, the nature of game writing is such that a sample containing one's loveliest, most well-wrought written work does not serve as proof of their ability to produce in context.

Inevitably, perhaps, programs' reputations will solidify as more and more students graduate and enter the industry, evincing what effective CGD should look like. It is my hope that programs form identities, also. Rather than seeking the "right" way to produce graduates with high employability, programs' faculty could build culture that leads to particular styles and approaches to the design process. Instead of getting students "in the front door" of the industry, we might focus on their growth as creators, thinkers, and communicators.

The Way Forward

Basing curriculum design and instruction on research, rather than on generalized assumptions regarding industry trends and practitioners' anecdotes, adds value to the students' CGD education. Beyond benefiting our students, developing sound, evidence-based pedagogy helps ensure that CGD programs stay relevant in an environment where more affordable, unbundled alternatives via online self-instruction in the technological tools of the trade (Selingo, 2015) call the value of a traditional college degree into question. What can we CGD educators teach you that the internet cannot?

A pedagogy receptive to industry influence and collaboration, but focused on sound instructional principles, is the way forward. Charting that path is easier said than done. This is the purpose of the research study behind this book: leveraging scholarship and research in order to develop effective pedagogy that prepares students for the game industry.

Though the purpose of my original study was to explore and enhance game writing pedagogy, its key findings reverberate across subdisciplines in the relatively young field of CGD in higher education. This model of student progression, in combination with the process-oriented, roles-based approach to pedagogy called for in this study, presents a tool for CGD faculty and programs to use for shaping instruction and curricula flexible enough to keep pace with a constantly changing industry, while also incorporating best practices in teaching and learning.

References

Aarseth, E. (2002). The dungeon and the ivory tower: "Vive la difference ou liaison dangereuse?" *Game Studies, 2*(1), 56–76.

Ashton, D. (2010). Productive passions and everyday pedagogies: Exploring the industry-ready agenda in higher education. *Art, Design & Communication in Higher Education, 9*(1), 41–56. https://doi.org/10.1386/adch.9.1.41_1

Brathwaite, B., & Schreiber, I. (2011). *Breaking into the Game Industry: Advice for a Successful Career from Those Who Have Done It* (1st ed.). Cengage Learning PTR.

Davidson, D. (2010). Games by degrees: Playing with programs. In *Beyond Fun: Serious Games and Media* (pp. 22–27). ETC Press. https://doi.org/10.1184/R1/6686723

Dille, F., & Platten, J. Z. (2008). *The Ultimate Guide to Video Game Writing and Design*. Lone Eagle.

Extra Credits. (2012, September 20). *On Game Schools—How to Find a Good Degree—Extra Credits*. https://www.youtube.com/watch?v=nmdGZk-fF98&index=5&t=381s&list=PLMjJwIszh6zXH3O_N2LbBHk_6cG6qESjr

Higher Education Video Game Alliance. (2015). *Our State of Play: Higher Education Video Game Alliance Survey 2014–2015*. http://glsstudios.com/hevga/wp-content/themes/hevga_theme/assets/2015_HEVGA_Survey_Results.pdf

Newman, J. (2013). *Videogames* (2nd ed.). Routledge.

Selingo, J. J. (2015). *College (Un)bound: The Future of Higher Education and What It Means for Students* (Reprint edition). Amazon Publishing.

Tripp, S., Grueber, M., Simkins, J., & Yetter, D. (2019). *Video Games in the 21st Century: The 2020 Economic Impact Report*. https://www.theesa.com/wp-content/uploads/2019/02/Video-Games-in-the-21st-Century-2020-Economic-Impact-Report-Final.pdf

2 Game Writing in Contexts

Effective writing instruction should focus on what we want students to do rather than what we want them to know (Russell, 2001). Designing and teaching courses in game writing requires an understanding of what game writers do. That is what I set out to do, unaware how difficult it would be to identify the work of game writers within a game—let alone what game writers actually do day to day.

This chapter situates game writing in three separate but related contexts: the game industry, computer game design (CGD) programs in higher education, and my approach as an educator-researcher. A selective literature review of sorts, I provide an overview of what game writing and game writers look like through these conceptual lenses. I also discuss how I designed and ultimately conducted my research, in hopes that others may extend or emulate that work.

Industry Context

Investigating game writing requires a look at the game industry, generally, and where game writers are situated in the design and production process. To accommodate varying levels of prior knowledge, I'll attempt to paint a picture of game design and development in a few meager paragraphs with the disclaimer that this painting is more stage backdrop than gallery masterpiece.

Role Confusion

For those outside the industry, there is often confusion about the roles and tasks of game designers versus those of game writers, fueled by a common misconception that game writing and game design are the same discipline. Much of this confusion stems from difficulties explaining the role of the game designer to those outside the industry.

DOI: 10.4324/9781003277668-2

Game writer and game designer are distinct roles. Richard Dansky, Manager of Design at Red Storm Entertainment and Central Clancy Writer at Ubisoft, puts it like this: "Whereas the game writer's role is chiefly to guide, develop, and script the narrative of the game, the game designer's role is to guide, develop, and document the gameplay" (Dansky, 2007, p. 20). Some hold this distinction as continually blurring line, but understanding the difference is key in defining game writing. Game design, while often employing written communication as a tool, requires a diverse set of skills ranging from mathematics and probability to understanding consumer and market behavior. Very simply, game design is the process of creating a game's rules and content followed by documentation and description of the necessary technical elements that deliver the experience (Bates, 2004; Schell, 2008). That's right. Game design starts with a document, not a computer; it starts with words, not lines of code.

The product of this initial process is a game design document—often just design doc or GDD—that serves as the backbone of the project's development (Bates, 2004; Peterson, 2004; Rouse, 2004; Saltzman, 2004; Tschang, 2007). The GDD is a living document that members of the team refer to and often edit as the production process moves forward. After the concept for the game is outlined, all aspects of the development, from gameplay mechanics, user interface, weapons, world descriptions, and technical data, are added (Newman, 2013). Stated another way, the game designer is a writer, but not the game writer (Dansky, 2007).

Like many industry practices, "there's no official 'right' way to write one of these" design documents (Saltzman, 2004, p. 215), as needs vary between studios and projects. There's no standard format for the GDD, just a shared understanding of its massive scope and importance. Once the partially initiated laypersons learn of the GDD, that game design starts on paper, confusion sets in: "If the backbone of game design is writing, then game writers must be those in charge of the process, right?" Not so fast.

The nuance of roles aside, what should be clear is the need for ample writing instruction in CGD. Too many disciplines rely on general composition courses, usually English 101, to take care of writing instruction. There seems to be an assumption that writing skills develop naturally as students gain content knowledge. A greater focus on writing throughout a curriculum reaps benefits for all aspects of a student's education. Unfortunately, many instructors assign writing tasks without any instruction on the process of creating that work. Worse still are those instructors who assign writing and assess it without paying any attention to effectiveness—the student writes to simply demonstrate knowledge rather than to communicate.

If the novelty of CGD affords us the opportunity to rethink/reshape our approach to the student experience, we would be remiss to consider some of the fundamental academic skills that have been lost in the past decades. I am biased on this, as a former composition and as someone active in writing across the curriculum initiatives, but that doesn't mean I'm wrong.

Industry Inertia

The need for skilled writers in the game industry is not a new development, even if that need has not been widely recognized. Stephen Jacobs (2004) highlighted the importance of story and writing for the medium, saying that "the industry will need to learn how to identify, grow, and nurture [professional game writers] if digital games are to move to the next level" (p. 33). According to Norman (1999), industry advances in technology alone will not move video games to their ultimate potential. The medium "must move beyond computer science and art to simply code games and make them look good" (Salmond, 2016, p. 24).

The writer is a very small part of the larger system of game production, but conversations surrounding the need for quality story content and strong writing continue to evolve in the industry and among consumers. Games historian Mark Wolf (2008) offered some context:

> Most video games are oriented around story (at times very weak), but the adaptation of narrative to an interactive medium in which players act and make decisions has both placed limitations on storytelling as well as opened new possibilities.
>
> (p. 304)

Many game writers admit that the limitations placed on game writing by technology and its role in the hierarchy of development have resulted in inferior narrative content. Given the continued success of the medium, the minimal resources dedicated to game writing may seem justified.

The challenges surrounding game writing have origins alongside the very beginnings of the video game industry, where development and production have vacillated between the poles of art and technology since the 1960s (Wolf, 2008). The evolution of the game industry has been one of technology, not entertainment. According to Newman (2013), most game industry marketing tended to focus on the performance of hardware and software rather than on the player experience.

Even today with games firmly established as a major force in the entertainment industry, and consumers demanding innovative content, the demand for "innovative stories" is less explicit. Risk-averse publishers in the AAA game industry are often accused of following formulaic models when it comes to content creation, prioritizing projects that tie into existing media or seek to expand the success of previous titles (Newman, 2013). Though affected by nuanced demands in development and production, *sequelitis* is real.

Beyond the balance sheet, historical factors influence the precarious place of game writing. To a casual observer, and likely to most game enthusiasts, the history of games tells a story of advancing technology. More advanced tech allows for sharper graphics and greater freedom in gameplay, making major milestones in the medium tied technological performance rather than artistic expression. Understandably, the things players can see, hear, and do in a game garner the most attention—my research participants would readily agree—so the game writer has remained in the backseat of this drive toward innovation.

While the importance and impact of skilled writing in game development have been demonstrated by numerous authorities, old doubts regarding the need for narrative content in games still linger. Common thinking in the industry insists that game writing must be compelling, yet disposable (Stoddard, 2016), as many narrative heavy elements like voice-acted dialogue of cinematic cutscenes are often muted or skipped over by players. For some, the presence of traditional creative writing in games, such as scripted dialogue and cinematic cutscenes, is thought to break the players' immersion in the experience, removing players' ability to interact with the game world (Rouse, 2004). Game writers navigate their day-to-day work with the knowledge that some of their contributions may be entirely neglected by the audience. This underlying debate regarding the role of story and writing in games should inform any inquiry into the practices of industry writers.

Given the challenges of writing for a developing medium with few established practices and the industrialized nature of game development, successful game writers must be flexible and work quickly in high-pressure environments (Chen et al., 2008), adopting an approach more akin to problem-solving (Heussner et al., 2015) than artistic expression through text. Often, the final task for many game writing jobs is documenting the process for the next group of writers to come on board (Chandler, 2007). Over time, though, the collective experience of game writers may approach standardization as individuals migrate from one studio to another (Peery, 2016). Rules for writing in the industry may not be apparent immediately, but research on how writers, game writers, operate in context has the potential to hasten the arrival of such rules.

Critical Reception

Strong writing cannot fix a poorly designed game (Heussner et al., 2015; Skolnick, 2014), yet poor writing can have a negative impact on a game's sales and reception. Scholars and game journalists alike have found that engaging stories with clever writing can increase emotional impact and heighten players' sense of immersion (Bissell, 2010; Isbister, 2016). For decades, scholars and practitioners have called for game developers to utilize the skills of writers and storytellers to advance their medium (Brown, 2008).

Having evolved beyond its technology-focused roots, the game industry must now cater to consumers demanding innovative content (Norman, 1999; Salmond, 2016; Tschang, 2007). Games featuring strong writing have been undeniably successful over the past two decades, with five titles winning awards for both Best Narrative and Game of the Year at the Game Developers Choice Awards: *Star Wars: Knights of the Old Republic* (BioWare, 2003), *Half-Life 2* (Valve Corporation, 2004), *Fallout 3* (Bethesda Game Studios, 2008), *Uncharted 2: Among Thieves* (Naughty Dog, 2009), and *The Last of Us* (Naughty Dog, 2013) (*Game Developers Choice Awards*, 2021). An even greater number of titles have been nominated for awards in both categories in that time span.

Current industry trends indicate an increased appreciation for story content in games. This appreciation does not seem to have overcome historical contentions or elevated the game writer's status, as these contributions are often still seen as an afterthought. Though quality writing in games has demonstrated value in terms of critical reception and sales figures, the industry still does not fully understand the value of game writers and game writing. This is evidenced by hiring practices that rely on adding freelancers to nearly completed work, or marketing that focuses on performance and graphics rather than on narrative content.

"…Because Nobody Ever Said, 'Oh, But the Story's too Good.'"

One of my study participants summed up the situation with great clarity. After a terrific conversation where we touched on everything from photography to Shakespeare—you'll hear more of our conversation later on—I asked Henry if there was anything else he'd like to add. Without hesitating:

> The other thing, the point that I often make [...] game narrative is cheap—really, really cheap. Compared to every other aspect of making a game, we are one of the least expensive parts that go into make a game, one of the least expensive departments. We don't have many staff. We don't need lots of expensive equipment. We generally can turn things around fairly quickly. We are incredibly cheap [...] compared to every other aspect of making a game.
>
> But we have an enormous impact on people's perception of the game, and especially critics' perception of the game. They will pay attention to the narrative. They will discuss it. Again, if it's good, they may not even mention it, but if it's bad, you can be sure they will. And not in a good way. You know, it's that whole thing about if you do a good job, nobody notices. If sometimes you do a bad job, then people notice. It's the thankless task.
>
> But that all matters, and like I say, we are incredibly cheap part of the process, but we have a huge impact on how a game is perceived. And so that's the argument that you can always use, as a young writer, especially, to push for better writing and for more emphasis on game narrative, because nobody ever said, "Oh, but the story's too good."

Though the importance of game writing has been historically marginalized in game development, there are signs that the industry is changing. The increasing importance of story and clever writing in games makes the unique skills of the game writer essential to the production process. Companies such as BioWare, "who have indulged the writing process," have created some of the most innovative and socially engaged work to date (Bissell, 2010), not to mention some of the innovative narrative that has come from indie studios in the past decade.

Game Writers Writing about Themselves

Except for a few academic references used as touchstones, the literature discussed below constitutes a wide sample from the trade press books on game writing and narrative design that are widely read by aspiring game writers. These are the kind of texts that engaged when I started teaching in CGD, looking for books with accessible content for the undergraduate level with structures conducive to teaching in a semester.

There is little agreement when it comes to the specific roles or tasks of game writers in production. Suckling and Walton (2012) present a humorous take on the situation, stating that game writers are sometimes known as "Story Medics, Story Robots, Script Monkeys, and sometimes just the Words Person" depending on the studio (p. 79). Often, these writing tasks may appear to play only a small role in the player's experience, but they are no less vital to the overall experience. Table 2.1 presents some common tasks of industry game writers found across these texts (Bateman, 2007; Chandler, 2007; Heussner et al., 2015; Suckling & Walton, 2012).

While many of the tasks referenced in Table 2.1 seem far removed from traditional ideas regarding creative writing—generating copy for the game's packaging to promote physical sales and writing press-release-style articles for trade publications—the skillful execution of the above should not be overlooked. Heussner et al. (2015) stated:

> Without [skilled writing], the quality of the game will suffer. And if it's done in a perfunctory way, players will either notice or just plain not care. Writing the "small stuff" well can be incredibly rewarding, particularly when players notice and discuss what they've seen.
>
> (p. 12)

Table 2.1 Common Tasks of Game Writers in the Industry

Overall Story/Plot Development	Iteration Response	Establish/Watchdog Tone
History and backstory	Story-related voiceover (V.O.) writing	Editing/polishing written content
Writing outlines and treatments	Narrative Design	Writing scripts, and script doctoring
Back of box copy	Website content	Articles for trade publications
Developer blogs	Character blogs	Media Tie-Ins
Story (sometimes)	Teaser fiction	World "bibles"
Character descriptions	Marketing	In-game artifacts
Cutscenes and scripted events	Editing for content authenticity	

Tasks of this kind are often the responsibility of entry-level writers in the industry, so writing them well is necessary for professional success (p. 11).

Game writing has only been considered a professional practice for a few decades (Peery, 2016). Assigned little importance in the past, game writing tasks fell to either whichever member of the development team was available or a professional writer added to the team very late in the development process (Novak, 2011; Peery, 2016; Pratchett, 2007; Skolnick, 2014). According to Tom Bissell, writer on *Gears of War: Judgement* (People Can Fly & Epic Games, 2013):

> The writer is someone who only occasionally steers the story ship during the game development process […] so much of it is responding as the game design stuff changes, and figuring out how to ground some pretty absurd gameplay hook in a plausibly fictional context. And that's the fun part. It's also the hard part.
>
> (As quoted in Suellentrop, 2013, n.p.)

There are many other "horror stories" about writers being abused by studios (Bissell, 2010). Not only do the expectations for a game script shift with advancing technology, but they must also factor in player freedom, often by writing content that aligns with multiple choices and actions over hours of gameplay (Dansky, 2007).

Though video games offer much more than just a story to players, an inconsistent or poorly executed story can hinder success. The "game writer" is best equipped to ensure that success (Skolnick, 2014). The emerging role of "narrative designer" may be a sign of how important story is becoming in the modern game industry.

CGD/Higher Education Context

Not bound by decades of historical influence or demanding production schedules, the role of game writing in CGD is more flexible. By embracing the increasing importance of story in video games and reflecting it in course and curriculum design, CGD programs can be uniquely beneficial to students seeking employment in the game industry. Additionally, as design documentation and other writing are done by team members involved in all facets of game development (Novak, 2011; Peterson, 2004), including industry-relevant writing instruction is valuable to all students in CGD, not just those seeking employment as game writers. Though in the past many in the game industry questioned the value of a CGD degree (Dille & Platten, 2008; Hoekstra, 2003; Mencher & Crosby, 2003), others believe candidates with college degrees have an advantage due to better writing, social, and time management skills (WatchMojo.com, 2017).

The book you read now all started with a desire to teach game writing effectively. An adjunct instructor preparing my first class for the CGD department, I reached out to one of my new colleagues to start my path to understanding game writing. The colleague, a seasoned AAA industry veteran, was happy to help. I approached:

From your experience, what should I be teaching in this game writing class?

I guess just a mix of screenwsriting and lore, with some of that Hero's Journey stuff in there somewhere.

That was his best advice, and it was sufficient for me to start designing and teaching the course. As a fan of video games myself, I knew there must be more to game writing than that.

"There's Nothing like Game Writing."

Video game writing is a hybridization of screenwriting, creative writing, and technical writing that is evolving into a new area of expertise and study (Peery, 2016). Traditional writing genres, ranging from composition to poetry, can be found in game writing, but rather than communicating a single author's vision to the audience, game writing serves to enhance the other elements of the player's experience (DeMarle, 2007; Sheldon, 2013).

The texts meant for instructive use that I found (Bateman, 2007; Chandler, 2007; Despain, 2009; Dille & Platten, 2008; Heussner et al., 2015; Sheldon, 2013; Skolnick, 2014) were based primarily on professional anecdotes. Lee Sheldon (2013) prefaced his book *Character Development and Storytelling for Games* with, "You hold in your hands most of what I know about writing for games" (p. xiv). Wendy Despain's (2009) collection on writing for video game genres is humorously prefaced as the industry-veteran authors' alternative to "drowning our sorrows and crying in our beer" (p. xiv).

While useful, these anecdote-based accounts fail to identify and expand upon the key functions and skills of game writers. Chris Bateman (2007) stated in *Game Writing: Narrative Skills for Videogames*:

> Despite the publication of many books about narrative in games, very little attention has been paid to the actual skills used by people working in the field of game writing. As a result, most discussion tends to be in abstract terms, and the pragmatic skills required to construct game narrative and dialogue are frequently overlooked entirely. In the absence of continuity of knowledge regarding the skills being used, the craft of game writing has lacked a clear definition.
>
> (p. xxv)

This study aims to identify the functional competencies of game writers, potentially addressing definitions of game writing in the process.

The game writing community's attempts to define their own practices are understandably limited in terms of scholarship—as is true for most professions. One widely held sentiment surfaces throughout the literature and pervades the industry: there is nothing else like game writing (Bateman, 2007; Chandler, 2007; Dansky, 2007; DeMarle, 2007; Heussner et al., 2015; Sheldon, 2013). Statements like this signify the limitations of relying on these trade press publications as a scholarly assessment of the field. The concept of writing as a loosely defined set of interrelated tasks and processes is now common in higher education.

Implications for Instruction

According to writing researcher Paul Prior (2003), "the writing process takes place in a structure of participation; tracing it involves examining who is involved in making the text and in what ways" (p. 170). Teaching writing with a focus on process, rather than on product, is so widely accepted that "it may be difficult to imagine alternative instructional approaches" (De La Paz & McCutchen, 2016, p. 33).

CGD programs may decide that writing the narrative content of games is not a priority, but importance of game design docs illustrates the value of writing in the industry and indicates a real need to emphasize writing in CGD curricula. According to Peterson (2004), "Game programmers and designers usually generate all the documentation associated with a game" (n.p.); therefore, strong writing skills are valuable to students seeking employment in the game industry, regardless of their intended role.

Offering a perspective from composition studies, Brandes Stoddard (2016) further explained the roles of the industry writer:

> Writing for games, whether as a matter of design or development, consists of essentially five branches of composition. The importance of these branches varies for each individual role within a company, and for the type of game the company makes. With lots of room to dispute the boundaries between them, the categories might be identified as technical or instructive writing, brief evocative writing, dialogue, flavor text, and plot or overarching narrative writing.
>
> (p. 339)

While Stoddard's contribution is useful to draw parallels between game writing and existing disciplines, his summary of these roles does not constitute the whole of professional game writing. Beyond incorporating the context and settings where game writing is practiced, its situation as just one subdiscipline in the medium should be considered when seeking its definition.

Aspiring creative writers in all established mediums must develop the fundamental skills necessary for writing compelling content, while also understanding the standard formatting necessary for presenting that work to relevant audiences. Unlike the writing produced in other entertainment industries, game scripts do not follow a standard format (Bateman, 2007; Chandler, 2007; Despain, 2009; Heussner et al., 2015; Peery, 2016). This presents a challenge to students aspiring to writing positions in the game industry, as successful applicants must demonstrate not only that they can write but that they can write for games (Dansky, 2007).

Put another way, writers in other narrative genres can produce work that closely resembles the genre they aspire to; game writers must devise a way to demonstrate their skill in various modes of writing. Working alone, aspiring screenwriters can create a screenplay, fiction writers can write a short story, but game writers do not have that same affordance. Students with writing credits on functioning games have a clear advantage when entering the field, as these credits demonstrate both the writing ability and tool proficiency preferred or even required for junior game writing positions (Heussner et al., 2015). The project courses and emphasis placed on portfolios in CGD programs provide a benefit to students in that regard, allowing them an outlet to demonstrate skills relevant to game writing.

Definitions and Perceptions of Game Writing

The authors of trade press books on game writing define their field by juxtaposing it with common ideas about creative writing likely driving the sentiment that "there is nothing else like game writing." This sentiment is shared by some other writers in academe. In his book, *Uncreative Writing: Managing Language in the Digital Age* (2011), Kenneth Goldsmith asserted that the field of creative writing is stuck on perpetuating the incorrect notion of the original artist in writing. Goldsmith indicated that this attitude limits the potential of creative writing in the digital age. Others, like Mayers (2005), highlighted university creative writing programs' common refusal to theorize about the ways creative work operates. As a result, potentially valuable qualitative studies of these practices remain non-existent.

Educator-Researcher Context

I had taught game writing for a few semesters with some success relying on those industry-borne texts and following the "mix of screenwriting plus some Hero's Journey stuff" model. My background as an educator gave me the tools to teach classes that were valuable to students, even if they failed to approach what game writing was "actually." My scholar self still wanted to define game writing and that required a conceptual framework.

> Early in my study, having just scrapped a load of useless data, I felt stuck. In my office, struggling to find the literature that could help shape things, I sprang from my chair in frustration to peruse my bookshelf once again.
>
> Eureka! Several of the sources that became part of my literature review had been sitting there for a decade. Things that I had learned and forgot. As I browsed, I realized that some of these concepts remained at the core of my teaching and scholarly interests—I failed to reflect and took them for granted. Fortunate for me, the bookstore's offer to buy them back was not worth the trouble. Had they offered more than a few dollars, who knows where I would be now.

Some of my influences were things I learned in preparing for the composition classroom a decade earlier, long since forgot. Other aspects of my conceptual framework were simply big ideas that had been floating around in my mind. I introduce these concepts below to provide context.

Cultural-Historical Activity Theory (CHAT)

Despite romantic notions of AAA games being developed in basements by small groups of talented, enthusiastic friends, "It is important to consider the mass production of games and the industrial process that makes their production possible, since both their aesthetic form and their consumption are influenced by this overarching structure" (Egenfeldt-Nielsen et al., 2015). CHAT is a useful framework for analyzing the various aspects of game development, as it is "practice-based and practice-oriented," focusing on "tool-mediated actions by collective actors as well as socioeconomic relations within and between institutional contexts over time" (Foot, 2014, p. 344).

Several scholars have extended Vygotskiĭ's (1978) model of activity theory in the last 30 years—Engeström (1999), Foot (2014), Nardi (1996)—but the underlying theory focuses on three central ideas:

• Humans act collectively and learn by doing, communicating in and through activities.
• Humans make, use, and adapt tools—literal and conceptual—to learn and communicate.
• The community is central to making and interpreting meaning in all forms of learning, communicating, and acting.

CHAT research has been applied to many fields, ranging from drama production and drug addiction to computer-mediated activities and language acquisition (Engeström, 1999; Nardi, 1996). It aims to advance ways of thinking about professional practices, shaping or reshaping them in context, and developing related teaching strategies and curricula (Foot, 2014). The CHAT framework is valuable for game development, as it provides a chance to look at how the development teams in different departments interact to produce a game.

Specifically, CHAT is conducive to defining the processes and the conditions for attaining concrete goals in a complex system, while also factoring in the ever-present dynamics of power, money, culture, and history (Foot, 2014). Useful for my purposes in its ability to isolate and analyze complex and evolving professional practices (Foot, 2014), CHAT studies often highlight contradictions and tensions within an activity system. Once identified, these tensions are treated as places where innovation can emerge and lead to transformational learning across the entire system or organization (Engeström, 1999). In terms of game development, CHAT studies have the potential to provide insight about the ways different departments and teams communicate with each other, leading to more efficient work.

Given the complexity of game development, complicated by poorly defined roles and a lack of standard practices (Newman, 2013), CHAT provides a valuable framework for addressing the topic of this study. CHAT's attention to constraints within a system is also intriguing for analyzing the work of game writers who are tasked with the writing that serves to enhance or provide context for other elements of the player's experience.

My study does not attempt to rigidly define the evolving practices of game development. Rather, the focus is on the day-to-day work of game writers and the competencies required to succeed in those roles. However, ignoring the larger context of game development disregards the realities of this study's topic and misses opportunities to help the participants identify some of the contradictions they experience. Thus, drawing on the CHAT framework, this study seeks to contextualize findings in relationship to the effects of power, money, dynamics, and social structures within game development.

Rhetorical Genre Studies (RGS)

While seemingly oversimplistic, the strongest advice—that I cite multiple times in this text—for students wishing to pursue game writing is to demonstrate "not only that they can write, but they can write for games" (Dansky, 2007). This quotation is loaded for those familiar with rhetorical genre studies (RGS) who understand all writing as a process dependent on context.

Russell (2001) holds that effective writing instruction should focus on what instructors want students to do, rather than on what they want them to know. For many researchers, writing instruction should also provide students with an understanding of genre to prepare them for successful writing careers post-graduation (Bazerman & Prior, 2004; Devitt, 2000; Miller, 1984; Russell, 2001; Swales, 1990).

Relying on John Swales' (1990) working definition, this study categorizes genre in the following ways:

- Genre is a class of communicative events playing a vital role in game writing that encompasses both written and oral communication.
- The principal feature of the communicative events from which genre evolves is a shared set of purposes among individuals within a particular professional setting.
- Exemplars of a particular genre vary in their prototypicality.

To this last point, Swales identified a definitional approach and a family-resemblance approach. The latter focuses on loosely shared interrelationships rather than on a list of defining features. Swales' family resemblance approach to genre is useful in the context of the game industry not only for writing but for analyzing the relationships between all the moving parts required in game production.

RGS approaches embrace the dynamic nature of any writing situation. The game writing literature presents the lack of standard formatting as a limitation to learning the practices of game writing, but RGS researchers understand that all writing is situational. This means that the common notion of "There is nothing else like game writing" found in the industry-borne literature is a null point. Were the same logic that results in that sentiment applied to writing in other professional situations, it would be true to say no writing shared similarity.

The gap between academe and the industry is apparent in the game writing community's assumption of uniqueness. Exploring the processes of game writing in context serves the scholarly purposes of this study, while also presenting useful information for the field. Applying RGS concepts to analyze the practices of game writers is a key tool in challenging the current assumptions in the field.

Though not stated in terms of RGS, game industry veteran Raphael Chandler (2007) calls on game writers to attempt the same understanding of genre, in situ:

> Each game features its own development process and documentation standards, but by studying the way other developers interact with story design and by considering the needs of the project, the writer can create an appropriate format for dialogue that will be easily integrated into the games production process.
>
> (p. 135)

Rather than defining the genre of game writing as a set of shared formal components, Chandler asks the individual to actively construct one while engaged in the activity. This aligns with CHAT's view that the object of an activity is shaped and directed by the activity (Engeström et al., 1999).

Tacit Knowledge—Making the Implicit Explicit

One of the "big ideas" that informed my thinking was the importance of reflection; in particular, the concept of tacit knowledge. Donald Schön's work, *The Reflective Practitioner: How Professionals Think in Action* (2017), influenced my conceptual framework. I share his assumption that competent practitioners actually know more than they can say. Schön states:

> When we go about the spontaneous, intuitive performance of the actions of everyday life, we show ourselves to be knowledgeable in a special way. Often we cannot say what it is that we know. When we try to describe it we find ourselves at a loss, or we produce descriptions that are obviously inappropriate. Our knowing is ordinarily tacit, implicit in our patterns of action and in our feel for the stuff with which we are dealing. It seems right to say that our knowing is *in* our action.
>
> (p. 62)

Making tacit professional knowledge explicit is valuable to advancing any field, but it is particularly useful when exploring new fields with few standard practices. Capturing the game industry professionals' perceptions is a first step in challenging the assumption that "there is nothing else like game writing" (Hudson, 2021).

Even if tacit knowledge is made explicit—thoroughly investigated and analyzed—the educator-researcher's interpretation and eventual implementation into pedagogy is what matters. This challenge applies across higher education. Many instructors are hired not for their teaching, but for expertise in scholarship and research in their discipline. The assumption is that success in the discipline lends itself to successful instruction. In many cases they are effective, but the hidden knowledge they possess may never be operationalized into pedagogy.

CGD instructors who conceive of game writing, or any games-related subdiscipline, as a mere synthesis of relevant tasks common in the industry are not likely to produce anything more than a list of possible classroom activities. Those who are willing to experiment in the classroom and attempt new methods of instruction that challenge traditional notions of higher education can truly empower students (Hudson & Willis, 2019). Instructors who frame pedagogy in more abstract ways, such as these essential roles, are better able to develop effective methods of instruction regardless of perceived constraints of time or resources (Hudson, 2021).

As I am interested in developing an effective pedagogy in the emerging field of CGD, I see this study as a synthesis of factors affecting the game industry and the subdiscipline of game writing, specifically. The methods outlined here reflect the need for meaningful exploration in the field that incorporates established scholarship and research from other academic disciplines. Relying on phenomenology, capturing the game writers' perceptions of what they do is a first step in challenging the assumption that "there is nothing else like game writing."

Learning from Others—A Primer in Phenomenological Research

Qualitative research is nuanced and sometimes messy. Trying to capture the experience of game writers was more challenging than I thought at first. In hindsight, I realize that all of the literature on methodology was vital in designing and carrying out the research. What follows is some background on my methodology and methods for interested readers, perhaps those not familiar with qualitative research. I am by no means an expert, so I summarize them as dutifully as I can—again, the kind of thing you might see in Chapter 2 of a doctoral thesis.

The philosophical underpinnings of phenomenology are vital when developing a composite description of shared experience; any scholar writing a phenomenology "would be remiss to not include some discussion about the philosophical presuppositions of phenomenology along with the methods in this form of inquiry" (Creswell, 2006, p. 59). Basic philosophical stances on phenomenology hold that it describes the essence of the lived experience, rather than giving explanations about it (Moustakas, 1994), and that the experiences of the individuals involved are conscious ones (van Manen, 1990). A phenomenological text is descriptive, but it is also interpretive in that it mediates between the participants and the researchers, and between interpreted meanings and what those meanings indicate in the scope of a study (van Manen, 1990).

Following Maxwell's (2013) interactive approach to qualitative research design, this study views interview data as evidence to be used critically to test ideas and develop theory, rather than to seek observable, measurable data for making inferences and drawing conclusions. The interview data was collected to test ideas and assumptions in CGD education and the game industry. In pedagogy, this data may test the assumptions of course content and instructional methods of educators in CGD who have previously relied on personal experience or best practices in teaching. The findings of this study, or those of possible extensions, also have potential industry applications. A thorough exploration of the practitioners' tacit knowledge may lead to a deeper understanding of the functions of the actors within game studios. That understanding has the potential to enhance both collaborative creativity and efficiency in production.

Pragmatic Validity

Another important idea that became central to my conceptual framework was pragmatic validity; discovering it was a vital breakthrough in my research journey. In qualitative research, validity pertains to "the extent to which our observations indeed reflect the phenomenon or variables of interest to us" (Pervin, 2005, p. 48). There is no statistical test to run on interviews to see if the data is accurate. This study was conceived based on sound theoretical assumptions, reflecting my topic and purpose, and designed to produce knowledge that could ultimately benefit others, such as students, CGD programs, and industry professionals. Interviews were conducted honestly, using member checks and follow-up questions when appropriate, and were thoroughly analyzed after the fact.

A pragmatically valid qualitative account is one that contributes to practice instead of merely generating unequivocally verified knowledge (Flyvbjerg, 2001). For pragmatist researchers, "truth is whatever assists us to take actions that produce the desired results" (Brinkmann & Kvale, 2014). The character of the researcher is vital to pragmatic validity, so I state it clearly. Rather than exploring this phenomenon with respect to what is, my focus was on what could be. Pragmatic validity also demands that my research results in action; any judgments regarding the quality or effectiveness of my work will come in the application of my findings.

Designing the Study

As an educator-researcher, I am not an objective observer. My goal is to tell the story of game writers in a way conducive to enhancing pedagogy. A phenomenological approach of this kind attempts a deeper understanding of the meanings behind everyday experiences, while also offering plausible insights that allow others to understand those experiences more completely (van Manen, 1990). I took great care to make these interviews more than just interesting conversations for me to consider in my teaching.

"What Do You Do? How Did You Learn To Do It?"

After years preparation as a student and reviewing literature—what is referenced in this book is selective—my "official" research questions were deceptively simple.

- What functional competencies are required of professional game writers?

• To what educational experiences do game writers attribute the development of these competencies?

In even simpler terms: "What do you do? How did you learn to do it?" Answers to the former question were interesting and indeed confirmed that no two "game writer" roles appear the same. Answers to the latter proved even more interesting and useful for my purposes.

Participants were enthusiastic and explicit when answering the "What do you do?" question. Hearing firsthand about the daily tasks these game writers undertake allowed me to see how individuals regard these tasks. From writing marketing copy and in-game content, to taking meetings with external studio executives and directing voice actors, the array of possible tasks for which to prepare students would be beyond the scope of a university course—or even two, three, or four of them.

One of the benefits of carrying out this research myself was the ability to probe a little deeper throughout the interviews. A collated list of all the tasks from my data would not provide anything useful beyond evidence that game writers do a lot of different stuff. As the interviewer, a simple "Oh, cool. Can you tell me what that looks like?" can open pathways to interesting topics and allow me to test my own ideas and assumptions.

Participants' responses to my questions regarding "how" they learned to do these things generally began with a pause. Sometimes with a slight tilt of the head and gently wrinkled brow, other times with wide eyes of incredulity, most of these writers had not really thought about it before. In several cases, I broke silence by clarifying: "It doesn't have to be something you did in school. It could be anything." That seemed to make the question even harder to answer for some who, presumably, began thinking of all the possibilities. In these cases, the length of the pause seemed to correlate with the depth of the answer. Together, the co-creation of knowledge, seeking to unpack their tacit knowledge, was the key to this research endeavor.

These are great writers who understand audience; a public-facing interview for some trade publication would call for answers appropriate to that audience. Participants' identities were protected, so they did not have to worry about how their comments might be taken out of context. When conducting my interviews, I included questions regarding writers' practices as individuals and as members of a larger production process. I prompted participants to share specific instances in addition to the general impressions (i.e., "Tell me about a time when you…" or "If I were a fly on the wall, what would that look like?") in an attempt to gather rich data.

Challenges Researching the Game Industry

In the past, studies of game industry practices have been limited. McAllister (2005) and Tschang (2007) referenced the general lack of game studio access granted to researchers for fear of industrial espionage, making it more difficult to determine common practices for the benefit of practitioners and scholars alike. More recently, though, Michigan State University researcher Casey O'Donnell gained access to game studios for ethnographic observation. O'Donnell's book, *Developer's Dilemma: The Secret World of Videogame Creators* (2014), posited that factors beyond industrial espionage are at play:

> The industry's pervasive secrecy, though it does not veil the preproduction itself, is in some respect an attempt by developers and the industry to hold themselves apart, as distinct from other industries. It lends game development a mystique or desirability. The idea that, "This is not work like other people's work. This is not *real* work or *ordinary* work: This is *game development*" pervades the culture.
>
> (n.p.)

According to O'Donnell, this mystique is appealing for some employees seeking freedom in the workplace, but it also has negative consequences for those aspiring to enter the industry. Game writers' insistence on the uniqueness of the field may be another example of this phenomenon.

The steps taken to ensure anonymity in my study—giving pseudonyms to specific individuals, organizations, or products, including the participants, in addition to limiting specifics in demographic reporting given the close relationships within the game writing community—allowed participants to be honest and open in their responses. In cases where the interviewee responses began with, "Since this is off the record," it was apparent that anonymity protected identities, while likely offering richer data.

Data Collection

As opposed to ethnographic approaches that may provide more robust data on day-to-day work through observation, such as O'Donnell's (2014), this study relies solely on what the participants said about their work. The reporting of each interviewee's lived experiences is specific to their career path, beliefs, biases, and a host of other factors informing who they are as people, in addition to their professional selves. Shared in the form of reflection, and sometimes relying on a participant's perception of others, at a minimum, the responses are filtered through hindsight.

I conducted most interviews during industry conferences. The conference sites—I'm omitting specifics to help preserve anonymity—were optimal for recruiting, as I used the published conference session descriptions to target individuals with relevant experience. In some cases, these sites offered the unforeseen challenges of finding mutually convenient times, as we competed with conference programming, networking, and other social engagements. Interruptions complicated data collection at times, but it is my belief that the "out in the open" nature of the interview setting was well received by participants. While offering a few challenges for transcribing the recordings, these interruptions also helped recruit additional participants.

Getting people to sit down for an interview at a conference is difficult. Even when someone is interested, the moment you ask them to sign an informed consent can be a deal breaker. I realized that introducing the form as something "that means I have to protect your identity" was the way forward. Otherwise, that very official-feeling form can scare people off. An unexpected benefit of the public setting for most interviews—I always made sure the participant was comfortable with the exact location—was recruitment. The same "long time, no see" exchanges that occasionally interrupted led to "Who's interviewing you?" Many times, that led to unsolicited offers of participation. Again, game writers are a really supportive community.

I have found the game writing community to be very open to an apparent outsider. "I'm not asking for work, so people are happy to talk to me" is how I first summed up my conference experiences. The frenzied networking that happens at industry events is something to behold. I still find amusement observing the badge readers who barely make eye contact before their eyes track down your lanyard to see who you work for. In my case, those looking to network professionally often see a university and move on. In other cases, established industry folks seem genuinely interested to see what I do and why I'm there.

Good Questions Make Good Conversations

Taking a conversation from interesting to informative can be tricky. Incorporating insights from literature on qualitative research interviews actually makes it easier to have a casual, comfortable conversation that is also useful as data. Knowing what kinds of questions to ask is key. Informed by my literature review, I developed an interview protocol and attempted to follow it in each interview for consistency. The protocol—basically just an outline—consisted of presupposition questions, process questions, and necessary follow-up questions to clarify or seek greater depth to participant responses.

Presupposition questions assume that each interviewee has something to say about a topic (Patton, 2002). Direct questions regarding the knowledge, skills, abilities, and characteristics of game writers fell into this category (e.g., "Tell me about your favorite writer to work with."). Process questions concerned the meaning of activities, the influence of context on those activities, and the processes by which those activities occurred (Maxwell, 2013). Questions regarding the day-to-day activities of game writers fell into this category (e.g., "Describe what it looks like when you sit down to write" was usually followed by "How is your writing process different in the studio?").

I allowed each interview to inform and shape the next, taking handwritten notes on my in-field outline throughout each interview to guide my questions and ensure the major topics of interest were covered. These notes also highlighted possible follow-ups in situ, allowing me to honor the conversational nature of the interview and wait for an organic opening in the discussion, rather than interrupting my participant's train of thought for follow-up questions. The data generated by these handwritten memos aided in post-interview review and in generating possible themes for revising future interviews and for eventual data analysis. In some cases, follow-up interviews were conducted.

Analyzing the Data

Interviews are living conversations, not transcripts (Brinkmann & Kvale, 2014), so I interacted freely with the data throughout the process. As Miles et al. (2013) suggest, I coded my data both during and after data collection. Coding in situ ensured I covered those questions necessary to my project while avoiding unnecessary repetition that might break the flow of conversation. Before and after the data collection, I performed open coding (Moore et al., 2005) to identify the functional competencies and learning experiences that the participants attributed to their development.

I also coded for emergent themes, common sentiments, and any pointed views emphasized by the participants. Some examples of emergent themes included defining the profession, referencing specifics regarding formal education, emotional intelligence, the sophistication of the medium, and professional advice. Common sentiments ranged from the lack of standardized practices in the industry to the importance of valuing flexibility and collaboration over authorial intent. Pointed views were also highlighted throughout the coding. These included sentiments explicitly stated as vitally important, repeated multiple times, or imbued with emotional intensity. In some cases, these pointed views were shared post-interview, as the speaker felt they might be out of bounds for a dissertation but were still important to share.

Reflection: So What? (… and for Whom?)

Advice from professionals is valuable to instructors and students alike, but it often fails to recognize the day-to-day realities of higher education and best practices in teaching. My research seeks insights beyond the generalizations outlined in the game writing literature. I want to engage the tacit knowledge of these practitioners as evidenced in their recollections of experience, rather than focusing on what they might share with students aspiring to work in the industry.

My approach to this research is not only applicable to game writing; its methods are accessible to faculty researchers regardless of their academic background. Given the range of disciplines taught in CGD programs, not many faculty are likely to focus their research and/or creative activity on pedagogical research. Informed by a minimal amount of relevant scholarship, anyone can play the role of educator-researcher. The result will be enhanced pedagogy and, ultimately, a foundation of practice in CGD education.

References

Bateman, C. M. (2007). Preface. In C. M. Bateman (Ed.), *Game Writing: Narrative Skills for Videogames* (pp. xxv–xxvii). Cengage Learning.

Bates, B. (2004). *Game Design: Vol* (2nd ed.). Course PTR.

Bazerman, C., & Prior, P. A. (2004). *What Writing Does and How It Does It: An Introduction to Analyzing Texts and Textual Practices*. Routledge. http://search.ebscohost.com/login.aspx?direct=true&db=nlebk&AN=102221&site=bsi-live

Bethesda Game Studios. (2008). *Fallout 3*. [Xbox 360], Bethesda Softworks, U.S.A.

BioWare. (2003). *Star Wars: Knights of the Old Republic*. [Windows], Lucasarts Entertainment Company, U.S.A.

Bissell, T. (2010). *Extra Lives: Why Video Games Matter*. Pantheon Books.

Brinkmann, S., & Kvale, S. (2014). *InterViews: Learning the Craft of Qualitative Research Interviewing* (3rd ed.). Sage Publications.

Brown, H. J. (2008). *History, The Humanities and New Technology: Videogames and Education*. Routledge. http://site.ebrary.com/lib/alltitles/docDetail. action?docID=10292213

Chandler, R. (2007). *Game Writing Handbook*. Cengage Learning.

Chen, S., Suckling, M., & Toole, A. (2008). Writing in a team. In *Professional Techniques for Video Game Writing* (Vol. 1–0, pp. 73–86). A K Peters/CRC Press. http://www.crcnetbase.com/doi/abs/10.1201/b10640-9

Creswell, J. W. (2006). *Qualitative Inquiry and Research Design: Choosing among Five Approaches* (2nd ed.). SAGE Publications, Inc.

Dansky, R. (2007). Introduction to game narrative. In C. M. Bateman (Ed.), *Game Writing: Narrative Skills for Videogames* (pp. 1–23). Cengage Learning.

De La Paz, S., & McCutchen, D. (2016). Learning to write. In R. Mayer & P. Alexander (Eds.), *Handbook of Research on Learning and Instruction* (pp. 33–56). Routledge.

DeMarle, M. (2007). Nonlinear game narrative. In C. M. Bateman (Ed.), *Game Writing: Narrative Skills for Videogames* (pp. 71–84). Cengage Learning.

Despain, W. (2009). *Writing for Video Game Genres: From FPS to RPG*. CRC Press.

Devitt, A. J. (2000). Integrating rhetorical and literary theories of genre. *College English, 62*(6), 696–718. https://doi.org/10.2307/379009

Dille, F., & Platten, J. Z. (2008). *The Ultimate Guide to Video Game Writing and Design*. Lone Eagle.

Egenfeldt-Nielsen, S., Smith, J. H., & Tosca, S. P. (2015). *Understanding video games: The essential introduction* (3 edition). Routledge.

Engeström, Y. (1999). Communication, discourse and activity. *The Communication Review, 3*(1–2), 165–185. https://doi.org/10.1080/10714429909368577

Engeström, Y., Miettinen, R., Punamäki-Gitai, R.-L., & International Congress for Research on Activity Theory. (1999). *Perspectives on Activity Theory*. Cambridge University Press.

Flyvbjerg, B. (2001). *Making Social Science Matter: Why Social Inquiry Fails and How it Can Succeed again* (S. Sampson, Trans.). Cambridge University Press.

Foot, K. A. (2014). Cultural-historical activity theory: Exploring a theory to inform practice and research. *Journal of Human Behavior in the Social Environment, 24*(3), 329–347. https://doi.org/10.1080/10911359.2013.831011

Game Developers Choice Awards. (2021, March 23). Game Developers Choice Awards. https://www.gamechoiceawards.com/archive

Goldsmith, K. (2011). *Uncreative Writing: Managing Language in the Digital Age*. Columbia University Press.

Heussner, T., Finley, T. K., Hepler, J. B., & Lemay, A. (2015). *The Game Narrative Toolbox*. CRC Press.

Hoekstra, K. (2003). Getting a job in the game industry. In B. Bates (Ed.), *Game Developer's Market Guide* (pp. 29–36). Premier Press.

Hudson, S. (2021). A research-based approach to game writing pedagogy. *Transactions of the Digital Games Research Association, 5*(3), Article 3. https://doi.org/10.26503/todigra.v5i3.124

Hudson, S., & Willis, B. (2019). Exploration: A dancer and a writer walk into a classroom. In A. James & C. Nerantzi (Eds.), *The Power of Play in Higher Education: Creativity in Tertiary Learning* (pp. 253–261). Springer International Publishing. https://doi.org/10.1007/978-3-319-95780-7_33

Isbister, K. (2016). *How Games Move Us: Emotion by Design*. The MIT Press.

Jacobs, S. (2004, November). Writesizing. *Game Developer, 11*(10), 18–24, 33.

Maxwell, J. A. (2013). *Qualitative Research Design: An Interactive Approach* (3rd ed.). SAGE Publications.

Mayers, T. (2005). *(Re)Writing Craft: Composition, Creative Writing, and the Future of English Studies*. University of Pittsburgh Press.

McAllister, K. S. (2005). *Game Work: Language, Power, and Computer Game Culture*. University of Alabama Press. http://ebookcentral.proquest.com/lib/gmu/detail.action?docID=438202

Mencher, M., & Crosby, O. (2003). Breaking into the game business. In B. Bates (Ed.), *Game Developer's Market Guide* (pp. 15–28). Premier Press.

Miles, M. B., Huberman, A. M., & Saldaña, J. (2013). *Qualitative Data Analysis: A Methods Sourcebook* (3rd ed.). SAGE Publications, Inc.

Miller, C. R. (1984). Genre as social action. *Quarterly Journal of Speech, 70*(2), 151–167. http://mutex.gmu.edu/login?url=http://search.ebscohost.com/login.aspx?direct=true&db=ufh&AN=13147541&site=ehost-live

Moore, D. T., Krizan, L., & Moore, E. J. (2005). Evaluating intelligence: A competency-based model 1. *International Journal of Intelligence and CounterIntelligence, 18*(2), 204–220. https://doi.org/10.1080/08850600590911945

Moustakas, C. (1994). *Phenomenological Research Methods*. SAGE Publications, Inc. https://doi.org/10.4135/9781412995658

Nardi, B. A. (1996). *Context and Consciousness: Activity Theory and Human-Computer Interaction*. MIT Press.

Naughty Dog. (2009). *Uncharted 2: Among Thieves*. [PlayStation 3], Sony Computer Entertainment, U.S.A.

Naughty Dog. (2013). *The Last of Us*. [PlayStation 3], Sony Computer Entertainment, U.S.A.

Newman, J. (2013). *Videogames* (2nd ed.). Routledge.

Norman, D. A. (1999). *The Invisible Computer: Why Good Products Can Fail, the Personal Computer Is So Complex, and Information Appliances Are the Solution* (Reprint edition). The MIT Press.

Novak, J. (2011). *Game Development Essentials: An Introduction* (3rd ed.). Delmar Cengage Learning.

O'Donnell, C. (2014). *Developer's Dilemma: The Secret World of Videogame Creators*. The MIT Press.

Patton, M. (2002). *Qualitative Research and Evaluation Methods* (3rd ed.). Sage Publications.

Peery, J. (2016). Game writing in practice—MMORPG quests. In D. Eyman & D. Andréa (Eds.), *Play/Write: Digital Rhetoric, Writing, and Games* (pp. 347–362). Parlour Press.

People Can Fly and Epic Games. (2013). *Gears of War: Judgement*. [Xbox 360], Microsoft Studios, U.S.A.

Pervin, L. (2005). *Personality: Theory and Research* (9th ed.). Wiley.

Peterson, M. (2004). Why game documentation is essential to a satisfying user experience. *Usability Interface: The STC Usability SIG Newsletter, 11*(2), 1–6. http://210.240.189.214/gamedesign/resources/02_class/02_class2/00_game_paper/BIT094101/Why%20Game%20Documentation%20is%20Essential%20to%20a%20Satisfying%20User%20Experience.doc

Pratchett, R. (2007). The needs of the audience. In C. M. Bateman (Ed.), *Game writing: Narrative skills for videogames* (pp. 185–200). Cengage Learning.

Prior, P. (2003). Tracing process: How texts come into being. In C. Bazerman & P. Prior (Eds.), *What Writing Does and How It Does It: An Introduction to Analyzing Texts and Textual Practices* (pp. 167–200). Routledge.

Rouse, R., III. (2004). *Game Design: Theory and Practice* (2nd ed.). Jones & Bartlett Learning.

Russell, D. R. (2001). Where do the naturalistic studies of WAC/WID point to. *WAC for the New Millennium: Strategies for Continuing Writing-across-Thecurriculum Programs, 259*–298. http://files.eric.ed.gov/fulltext/ED454552.pdf#page=272

Salmond, M. (2016). *Video Game Design: Principles and Practices from the Ground Up*. Fairchild Books.

Saltzman, M. (2004). *Game Creation and Careers: Insider Secrets from Industry Experts* (1st ed.). New Riders.

Schell, J. (2008). *The Art of Game Design*. CRC Press. http://proquest.safaribooksonline.com/9780123694966

Schön, D. A. (2017). *The Reflective Practitioner: How Professionals Think in Action*. Routledge. https://doi.org/10.4324/9781315237473

Sheldon, L. (2013). *Character Development and Storytelling for Games* (2nd ed.). Course Technology PTR. http://proquest.safaribooksonline.com/9781435461048

Skolnick, E. (2014). *Video Game Storytelling: What Every Developer Needs to Know about Narrative Techniques*. Watson-Guptill.

Stoddard, B. (2016). Writing for games. In D. Eyman & D. Andréa (Eds.), *Play/Write: Digital Rhetoric, Writing, and Games* (pp. 339–346). Parlour Press.

Suckling, M., & Walton, M. (2012). *Video Game Writing: From Macro to Micro*. Mercury Learning & Information.

Suellentrop, C. (2013, March 19). Gears of War: Judgment, and the Writing of Its Narrative. *The New York Times*. https://www.nytimes.com/2013/03/20/arts/video-games/gears-of-war-judgment-and-the-writing-of-its-narrative.html

Swales, J. (1990). *Genre Analysis: English in Academic and Research Settings.* Cambridge University Press.

Tschang, F. T. (2007). Balancing the tensions between rationalization and creativity in the video games industry. *Organization Science, 18*(6), 989–1005. https://doi.org/10.1287/orsc.1070.0299

Valve Corporation. (2004). *Half-Life 3.* [Windows], Sierra Entertainment, U.S.A.

van Manen, M. (1990). *Researching Lived Experience: Human Science for an Action Sensitive Pedagogy.* State University of New York Press. http://site.ebrary.com/lib/georgemason/Doc?id=10588818

Vygotskiĭ, L. S. (1978). *Mind in Society: The Development of Higher Psychological Processes.* Harvard University Press.

WatchMojo.com. (2017, July 28). *Top 10 Tips for Getting into the Video Game Industry.* https://www.youtube.com/watch?v=3SH3CPJhthE&index=5&list=PLMjJwIszh6zXH3O_N2LbBHk_6cG6qESjr

Wolf, M. J. P. (2008). *The Video Game Explosion a History from PONG to Playstation and beyond.* Greenwood Press. http://mutex.gmu.edu/login?url=http://search.ebscohost.com/login.aspx?direct=true&scope=site&db=nlebk&db=nlabk&AN=218335

3 Approaching Game Writing/Writers

I write now with clarity afforded by reflection. The years-long span of designing my study and collecting data was not so clear-cut. At the time I was confident in the utility of my research, as new insights from my interviews informed my teaching. Put another way: if my goal was to better serve my students, that was happening long before the words of my dissertation appeared on the page.

Reviewing the first draft of this book, I felt that the voices of my participants were missing. At a loss for a more effective way to communicate their sentiments, what follows in this chapter is excerpted—with only minor alteration—from my doctoral thesis. It represents the end product of my making sense of the data, my thinking on paper to make my experience as a researcher useful to others. Let's see if it worked.

Purpose

This study seeks to identify the functional competencies of professional game writers and examine the educational experiences to which professional game writers attribute the development of their skills. The study's purpose is achieved through a phenomenological study exploring the lived experiences of game writers. Since the study reveals the processes and perceptions of writing in the game industry, rich data for potential extensions in future scholarship are developed. Studies of this kind provide valuable insight regarding working in industry contexts that, combined with teaching expertise, allow the faculty in CGD programs to enhance instruction to meet their learning outcomes and provide meaningful, professional preparation for their students.

DOI: 10.4324/9781003277668-3

This study is based on the following research questions:

* What functional competencies are required of professional game writers?
* To what educational experiences do game writers attribute the development of these competencies?

The following chapter presents the important findings from my study. All the interviews focused on my two research questions, which sought to identify the functional competencies of game writers and the learning experiences associated with those competencies. To encourage further exploration of relevant topics, the interviews were intentionally semi-structured.

While 13 interviews were conducted over the course of the study, the following findings focus on conversations with seven individuals. The other six interviews were excluded from these findings because three interviews conducted early in the study produced usable data but served as a pilot for revising the study's design, while another three interviews were conducted with volunteers who did not have sufficient studio experience to contribute meaningfully to the research questions.

The seven interviews included in these findings (see Table 3.1) were conducted with individuals currently working in the AAA games industry in writing-focused positions. These individuals have experience

Table 3.1 Breakdown of the Participants' Professional Experience

Pseudonym	Years in the Industry	Titles	Players	Studio Type	Platform	Other Genres
Margaret	10	5	3 million	AAA, Small	Console, Mobile, PC	Fanfiction
Micah	10	11	20 million	AAA	Console, PC	Comics, Fiction
Lou	<5	1	1 million	AAA	Console, PC	Fiction
Peter	16	49	>100 million	AAA, Small	Console, Mobile, PC	Comics, Non-fiction
Garreth	14	5	16 million	AAA	Console, PC	Screenwriting
Henry	10	14	>100 million	AAA, Small	Console, Mobile, PC	Comics, Fiction, Graphic Novels
Robert	8	7	>100 million	AAA, Small	Mobile	Playwriting, Screenwriting

with a variety of game types, from mobile and Facebook games to first-person shooters and AAA role-playing games. They have been given pseudonyms to protect their identities.

Participant Overview

The participants included in this study's findings have significant professional experience and have worked in the industry from under five to over sixteen years. Additionally, all seven maintain writing careers in different genres outside the game industry. Table 3.2 presents a collated list of the various job titles each has held.

Each section begins with a brief account of the setting of the interview and my relationship with the writer. Though many responses pertaining to my research questions overlap, I have included redundancies across the interviews where I believe notable differences of possible significance occur. While the same competencies were mentioned by some interviewees, the context in which they were described is different. To that end, I rely heavily on the natural language of the interviews to give readers a sense of each participant's personality. Where appropriate, rough definitions of certain terms, as used by the participants, are included.

For clarity, these findings adopt the term "sensemaking." While respondents used phrases like "help the player make sense of it all," the term sensemaking, as it is used in organizational science, seems applicable. Taylor and Van Every (2000) define sensemaking as the process through which circumstances are turned into a "situation that is comprehended explicitly in words and that serves as a springboard to action" (p. 40). As discussed in this chapter, the game writer plays the role of sensemaker by providing context for both the development team's collective vision of the story and the player's experience of the game.

Table 3.2 Combined Position Titles of Participants

Co-Head Writer	*Narrative Designer*
Designer	Producer
Franchise lead writer	Script doctor
Game writer	Story adaptation consultant
Lead designer	Story designer
Lead narrative designer	Story/world building consultant
Lead writer/translator	Writer
Narrative design consultant	Writer/world building

Three Essential Roles of the Game Writer

This study identified three essential roles that game writers play, in some capacity, across contexts. Although little uniformity exists across titles and roles in the industry (Bates, 2004; Newman, 2013), these roles encompass the array of tasks the game writer may perform in any given setting. Described below, these include the roles of wordsmith, sensemaker, and advocate.

Wordsmith

The game writer's focus is on execution rather than creativity. Completing the assigned tasks of game writing requires flexibility when crafting with text. From writing in-game content to blog posts and press releases, the game writer's ability to create text in many forms, according to specific requirements, and within the constraints of time and technology, is vital.

Sensemaker

The game writer seeks to understand the creative views of individuals in other subdisciplines to build a sense of ownership for the game's story from all those involved in the production. The game writer also provides context for the player. A greater focus in both areas is important as the medium grows in sophistication and continues to incorporate richer, more complex stories.

Advocate

The game writer champions the story vertically to the decision-makers and horizontally across the subdiscipline teams. Combining the game writer's skills in storytelling with his or her ability to communicate effectively, assuming the role of advocate allows the game writer to empower all members of the development team to create a story for the player to experience.

Five Areas of Competence/Functional Competencies

During the semi-structured interviews, the participants reported several functional competencies required for their industry-specific, writing-related tasks. In many cases, these competencies overlapped, sometimes varying in the degree of reported importance depending on their specific roles within the studio or elsewhere. As each conversation evolved, however, other topics relevant to this study surfaced.

To account for these variations, I have developed categories based on topics common across the interviews. Rather than highlighting the specific abilities, skills, knowledge, and characteristics associated with each task, these are grouped as areas of competence. Listed below, each area of competence encompasses a group of competencies required to support a productive career in game writing:

- Writing and storytelling—required to produce written text and generate engaging story content efficiently;
- Communication and collaboration—required to work effectively with other individuals in studio environment;
- Understanding systems and dynamics—required to perform functions at a high level within the limitations of production and technology;
- Tool proficiency—required to demonstrate the transfer of writing and storytelling skills to the tools, both technological and conceptual, of the industry; and
- Understanding play—required to create content for games by producing writing conducive to interactivity and allowing for player freedom.

For each interview, I share an overview of the participant's reported views on these areas of competence and associated learning experiences. Each section closes with additional thoughts of note for the reader and a conclusion that summarizes the major findings in context and provides some interpretation where appropriate.

"This Doesn't Have Anything to Do with Game Design."—Margaret

Margaret's responses stressed the importance of professionalism and flexibility in wordsmithing. In terms of learning experiences, Margaret made clear connections between her current role and academic experiences in research writing while also mentioning other college experiences that taught her vital soft skills. This was unique from other interviews, where those connections were not made explicit or referred to. In general, her responses offered advice to game design students, though once the interview was underway, the discussion highlighted several challenges game writers face on the job.

Margaret has worked in the game industry for ten years on five major titles experienced by over 3 million players. She also writes fanfiction. Her formal education consisted of a degree in English from a small, four-year liberal arts college. Although she did not intend to follow a career path in the game industry, she recalled that valuable learning experiences, such as serving as editor of a student literary journal and engaging in writing in her free time, contributed to her current success. She wrote on her own time for fun and recollected that the experience prepared her for the industry. At one point in the interview, Margaret stated that her preparation in the areas of competence came in seren-dipitous forms "and this doesn't have anything to do with game design."

Writing and storytelling. I began the interview by asking Margaret to describe her typical day. The list she provided echoed the literature regarding the many tasks given to game writers:

> So, I am [lead writing position] at [a studio], and what that title means varies greatly depending on the company. At my company, which is less than 100 people and sort of straddling the line be-tween startup and small company at this point, I write everything for [game title]. I, up until very recently, was writing everything for [another game title]. I assist Marketing with some content market-ing pieces and just copywriting on the rest of their materials. I do a lot of miscellaneous wordsmithing on other company projects. If designers need terms for items or abilities or stuff like that, I help them brainstorm and come up with the terms.

Margaret shared this long list with enthusiasm, rather than lamenting the chaos of playing so many roles at once. It is not atypical that "less than 100 people" is considered a small company in the game industry. Her use of the term "wordsmithing" also set the tone for our conversa-tion, as she continually framed the roles of game writer and narrative designer as those individuals who "use words to do stuff."

Regarding storytelling, Margaret was largely self-taught. Outside the hours she spent with academic and formal extracurricular writing in college—Margaret was also a tutor in the writing center—Margaret wrote fanfiction. She was self-deprecating in this admission, saying it might "seem lame and nerdy," but those side projects meant to be "just for fun" helped her land her first industry job. Margaret made it clear that she did not advise aspiring game writers to pursue fanfiction as a direct path to game writing in the industry but indicated that any practice writing in the voices of other authors, clearly and concisely, is valuable.

Margaret felt that these side projects required her to employ the skills she honed in academic writing. They also required her to prac-tice inhabiting the voices of other characters and mimicking other authors' styles. By focusing on specific writers' styles, she built important industry skills related to flexibility. She said, "if the writer changes between one part of the game to the next, or even one title to the next, the player should not be able to tell."

Communication and collaboration. Margaret described the typical process of her work as a narrative designer. First, she determines what the design team is "really" asking for. Next, she translates this to the writing team in whatever way it makes sense to them. In both cases, Margaret employs emotional intelligence to understand and effectively communicate with multiple audiences. The ability to bridge gaps in understanding between different teams is vital to Margaret's work.

The role of culture fit, an industry term connoting the preferred attitudes and social skills needed to function in a particular studio environment, is important to consider given the demanding and high-stress environment of game development. In fact Hewner and Guzdial's (2010) study of industry hiring practices found that some find technical skills secondary to elements of culture fit in making hiring decisions. Given the relatively small size of the game-writing community and the tight-knit nature of the industry as a whole, "being easy to work with" is vital in game writing. This was best exemplified by Margaret's response to my question, "What do you look for when hiring?":

> The first thing that I care about is you are a nice person who can take criticism, reacts well in situations, and is able to grow as a person and improve. That's what is most important to me. I would rather have someone who I need to teach a little bit than someone who's already perfect, but they're an [a**hole]. Because I can get that person where they need to go very fast if they're nice and easy to work with. I can't fix [a**hole]. I can't do anything about that.

This candid response did not seem born out of frustration; it was measured and matter-of-fact. In Margaret's view, interpersonal skills and basic professionalism are difficult to identify in applicants, though their importance is nearly equal to having writing-specific skills. Job postings are not likely to include "jerks need not apply" criteria for various reasons, so identifying and recruiting writers who possess both talents usually starts with seeking recommendations from peers. Combined with the volatile nature of game industry employment that involves developers moving from one project or studio to the next with some frequency, one's reputation can be even more significant than one's skill in their chosen subfield.

For Margaret, communication and collaboration also included work habits. In her view, the willingness to accept assigned tasks, a minimum amount of required copyediting—within reason—for all written work submitted, and simply "showing up ready to work" provide evidence of caring about the project and showing respect for the team.

Understanding systems and dynamics. For Margaret, understanding the workplace environment and studio dynamics means more than being a good team member. Mastering the systems of production within the studio is vital to her role as a storyteller. Several times in our interview, Margaret used the term "productive criticism" when discussing all phases of game writing tasks, rather than the term "constructive criticism." This was telling, as it related to Margaret's focus on pragmatism and matter-of-fact stances about what works during the development process.

When asked to expand on her use of the term, Margaret indicated that, in her view, productive criticism factored in the time-sensitive nature of the game writing process. Feedback should serve to enhance the game's story and the player's experience, but it cannot come at the cost of development. Consequently, the importance of understanding systems and dynamics is twofold. First, the game writer must understand the mechanics and interface of the game to write effective content. Second, the game writer must make choices that take the realities of production into account.

Tool proficiency. Related to understanding the mechanics of a video game, Margaret mentioned the importance of pen and paper games in teaching the roots of interactivity. She also stressed that in a competitive job market, aspiring game writers increasingly need to understand the digital side to demonstrate their writing skills, saying: "There are a 'bajillion' different tools out there for whatever your level of technical knowledge is. If you're also really good at scripting and stuff, you can just make your own game."

Understanding play. More than understanding the systems and dynamics involved in the game itself and production, the game writer must "figure out" the player experience on an emotional level. This empathy for the player is a major stumbling block for writers from other mediums who enter the game industry. Margaret discussed the need for honoring the player experience, saying:

> You have to let them shape their character how they want. You might have in your head, "Oh, I'm a badass." But maybe the person playing doesn't want to be a badass; they want to be a nice person. So, you have to give them a nice option. Maybe they want

to be devious; you have to give them a devious option. You have to think through all the potential experiences people want to have and provide those. And they all have to be satisfying. You can't try and subvert and be like, "Well, I really want people to do the badass route, so I'm only going to work real hard on that one and make that one good, and I'm going to make the other one [crummy] so that everyone will pick the other." You don't want to do that. You want to make every experience satisfying no matter which path they choose.

She concluded by advising that game writers must learn that "the player's experience is just as important as your art."

Margaret's associated learning experiences. I asked Margaret if she thought all these competencies could be learned on one's own, outside of higher education. She felt that learning all the necessary competencies alone is possible, but that college is valuable because of the things you learn unconsciously. Regarding the college experience, Margaret shared, "You constantly build muscles of writing, critical thinking, and communication along the way. When you sit down to write, those muscles are there even if they are taken for granted."

Margaret was explicit in her praise of academic writing's value, which she defined as "research papers and essays," holding that it builds all the skills mentioned above, in addition to other skills vital to her current success. Though game design was not part of her formal education, her college focused on writing-intensive courses.

Instead of seeing academic writing as just another chance to practice writing skills and "build muscles of writing," she highlighted the practical skills of time management and taking direction as defining features of her current pragmatic approach. Margaret reported that her senior thesis experience required her to budget time over long periods and develop flexibility regarding her thesis advisors' feedback. These experiences trained her for her situation in the game industry. The personality traits and work habits Margaret possesses, which have allowed her to embrace the game writing process, have foundations developed during her undergraduate career.

Margaret was clear that skill with tools comes from using them. She advised aspiring game writers: "You don't have to have my permission to try and write a game. You don't have to be paid to write a game. You don't have to have some special tool to write a game. Just write a game." She mentioned that demonstrating proficiency with these tools can come through the clever use of a word processor. Creating a conceptual tool for the interactive dialogue one might find in a game shows that proficiency. She also noted this as an opportunity to demonstrate one's understanding of specific voices and writing styles when applying for a position.

Margaret seemed to take her own tacit knowledge of these conventions for granted. When asked how one might learn these important skills, she was momentarily at a loss before indicating that any kind of nine-to-five job "would probably" teach the things one might need to know. She used the specific example of a bank teller, though she never held such a position. It appears that this tacit knowledge was obtained during Margaret's college experience. While her experiences as a dedicated student, writing center tutor, and editor of school publications might not seem directly applicable to the game industry, she developed valuable skills through these learning experiences that helped her succeed.

Thoughts of note. Margaret closed our interview by offering one final piece of advice for aspiring game writers, saying, "They need to learn that interactivity and the player's experience is just as important as your art." The specific word choice is notable. It is telling that she used the phrase "just as important," rather than "more important." The focus on interactivity and the player were common themes across the interviews. While Margaret echoed others' sentiments regarding pragmatism in game writing tasks, her view differed from those who framed the situation as the game writer's subservience to designers and players. While Margaret's approach is pragmatic and her language direct, this simple word choice indicates pride in her craft. Enhancing her own skills as a writer and storyteller by mastering the systems of production and doing all the "non-writing" work necessary of the position, Margaret's art is the player's experience.

Conclusion. Margaret's responses highlight the need for a baseline of professionalism in the game industry and present the value of a writing-intensive undergraduate education. She presents important aspects of the wordsmith and sensemaker roles, describing how the game writer must be able to craft words in any context asked of them. Important when considering game writing instruction, Margaret's sentiments align with DeVoss et al.'s (2010) call for writing instruction that helps students analyze the rhetorical situations and settings of writing to instill flexibility and strategic thinking across contexts. While not stated explicitly in our interview, Margaret's approach also highlights the importance of enthusiasm and diligence when approaching the work of a game writer, accepting the role of "the words person"

(Suckling & Walton, 2012). These qualities are framed differently by other interviewees but are common in this study.

"The Ability to Say, 'Yeah, All Right.'"—Micah

Micah's responses centered around the importance of skilled storytelling and efficient crafting of realistic characters and dialogue. He discussed the writers' sensemaking role at some length and included some examples that pushed his limits in doing so. Micah represents an experienced writing professional who moved into the game industry. His experience differs from Margaret's, and others, in that he is a career freelancer. This fact continually surfaced in data analysis and should frame the reading of this section.

Micah has worked in the game industry for ten years on 11 titles experienced by over 20 million players, mostly as a freelance writer. He has simultaneously continued a career writing comics and fiction. His formal education involved studying creative writing at a large state university. My interview with Micah was our first meeting. When preparing for the interview, I learned that Micah had significant experience in comics and considered it important to explore the ties between that medium and game writing.

Micah openly discussed his craft and professional experiences, carefully considering each question rather than sharing his general thoughts on career preparation. He offered significant details and insight with the assurance that details would be omitted to protect his identity. Generally, Micah presented game writing as a process of revision and iteration, sharing:

> I don't know if it's an accepted saying, but something that I've heard quite a few times in game writing [is], "we don't have time to do it right the first time, but we have time to do it five or six times."

Micah also noted his willingness to embrace the limited authorship perceived by some creative writers entering the industry. He attributed this stance to his career as a freelancer, citing that there are few better motivators than being able to pay the rent and buy food.

Writing and storytelling. Throughout the interview, Micah repeated that concision is a key skill necessary for meeting the demands of game writing. First, concision makes it easier for game writers to be creative within very strict parameters. Writing in comics, he said, is restrictive due to rigid page counts and panels, and sometimes even the size of speech balloons, but compared to game writing, comics are "nowhere near as restrictive." He offered an example:

For instance, a mobile game that I just worked on where the character interactions could be no more than like, five lines of dialogue and each line could only have 100 characters in it, and I had to convey the story that I came up with, so if it was complex, it was my own fault. But I had to convey all of the story in the game in these extraordinarily limited ways.

Conveying the most information in the fewest possible words is vital for a game writer's storytelling. It is also an integral part of navigating the demands of game development.

Concision also allows for greater iteration opportunities. Rather than a game writer bracing him- or herself for the next change handed down by designers, Micah pointed out that a fast writer creates space for more revision and iteration, with the result being more creative freedom. For any game, he said, "You need to be able to write convincing dialogue, from multiple points of view, really quickly, and then not be precious about it." In Micah's experience, the more concise this work is, the faster it can be produced, and the better the chance it can receive feedback. Many writers from other narrative genres perceive the restrictions of game development as a stumbling block that hinders creativity. Even though Micah was an experienced author in other mediums before entering the game industry, he was insistent that mastering the restrictions of game writing leads to more creative freedom.

Communication and collaboration. Several times throughout our interview, Micah referred to the game writer "making sense" of the player's action within the game. This also applied to making sense of the pivots in story direction presented by designers or of major changes made to particular levels. While Micah was used to thorough revision and collaboration with other subdisciplines in his comic writing, especially to find cohesion between the artist's vision and the writer's vision, writing tasks in a game studio were presented with fewer artistic nuances. In one of his earliest game studio experiences, Micah recalled being presented with an in-game scenario and directed, "Okay, write dialogue that makes sense and conveys what we want to convey."

More than the problem-solving and creativity required of bespoke writing, this sensemaking process requires the skill to understand the minds of others. It is possible that a high level of skill in this regard has been a key to Micah's success, as he has an ability to understand what designers and others are trying to convey even if it is not communicated clearly. I asked Micah if early studio experiences, such as the one referenced above, felt foreign or fundamentally different from previous writing experiences. He replied, "No, it didn't feel foreign. It's just one of the skills that the game writer has to have: being presented with a situation and adapting to it pretty much instantly."

Understanding systems and dynamics. Micah echoed the sentiments regarding the limited creative freedom and constant demands of the game writer's role found in the literature, and in other interviews, but framed it in terms of choosing battles. When asked for professional advice on entering the field of game writing, or for freelance writing in general, Micah said, "One of the most valuable skills that I've developed is the skill to say, 'Yeah, all right.'" He offered the following hypothetical scenario to describe this skill:

> If it's a rescue mission and then, all of a sudden, the player is not trying to rescue the daughter of [an] ambassador, all of a sudden, they're trying to rescue a decorated war hero, I say, "Yeah, all right. I'll make adjustments." Because all of the dialogue in that [scene or level] would change then, not just because of the circumstance but also because of the attitudes of the players.

It is worth noting that Micah understands his audience at multiple levels, as he attempts to write to enhance the player's experience, not just satisfy the design team. He also mentioned accepting that narrative and gameplay cohesion working out "just okay" is good enough if the team is satisfied.

Micah pointed out that the "yea, all right" skill comes with consequences at times; occasionally, the writer who says "yea, all right" must accept diminished quality of the story—diminished in the eyes of the writer, at least. He went on to say that this should not lead to discouragement or detract from the quality of the writing, but sometimes it means knowing the game experience could have been better for players.

Extending the militaristic metaphor, game writers must choose battles, but they do not determine the strategy or ultimate outcome of the war. During the development process, the goal is not always to win the war. Rather, the goal is to have it end so the game ships to the consumers on time.

Tool proficiency. Regarding the importance of tool proficiency, Micah was less adamant than some other interviewees, saying, "Well, it never hurts if you understand how to use some of the tools that a lot of game companies use." He found that discovering and honing the ability to write creatively is the primary skill a game writer needs. When he referenced tools, generally, Micah meant the conceptual tools of the writer. He recalled a unique phrase that a friend's father used repeatedly, "I swear to my time!" that he had not heard anywhere else and the meaning of which he was not even sure of. He mentioned that cataloging distinctive utterances such as this is "like putting tools in your toolbox."

Understanding play. Micah highlighted the importance of play when applying writing skills to games, as did most other interviewees. The common task of sensemaking requires an understanding of the player experience best achieved through play. Micah also mentioned the importance of understanding different kinds of games and gameplay.

As an example, Micah recalled being tasked with providing dialogue for a multiplayer role-playing game. The game's design and technical setup allowed the writers to use branching dialogue options and have the player answer questions, but they were discouraged from using these extensively because they did not adhere to the vision for the game. Micah shared, "The emphasis was on action because it had elements of a first-person shooter, so [the design team] didn't want the player just standing around talking all the time." Having played these action-heavy games himself, Micah recognized the player expectations for the genre and adjusted accordingly.

Micah's associated learning experiences. Micah's college education helped prepare him for a career as a writer, but it did not include any courses on game design or development. Making the shift to game writing is a challenge for some experienced authors, but Micah's experiences in other professional settings served him well. He mentioned that working with artists in comics prepared him for communicating with those in other subdisciplines, and that living and working as a freelancer helped him hone his "Yeah, all right" skills.

Having studied creative writing in college, Micah had some clear memories of workshop experiences. Asked to identify his favorite workshop experience, Micah mentioned the professor by name and explained:

> [...] And he said to the students, "Bring in some words, bring in a story, a chapter of a novel, a poem, a song that you wrote, just bring in something," and we would read the whatever-it-was, and then we'd all talk about it, and the insights that he had were kind of life-changing. And he was a poet, and he was so quiet and succinct. But he'd say something which would make so much sense.

Micah could not express why this kind of feedback was so useful. He only remembered that the format of the course, combined with a thoughtful professor, was more valuable than other classes that focused on more structured approaches to content and feedback. Given

Micah's discussion about a game writer having to work within limitations, it may seem contradictory that he valued the loosely structured approach to workshopping.

Micah's chief influences as a writer were comic books, and he analyzed and emulated their style in his own writing to improve his craft. In an aside, Micah mentioned that some people still use the term "comic book dialogue" derisively. The movie *Pulp Fiction* (Bender & Tarantino, 1994) presented an "aha" moment for Micah. Watching *Pulp Fiction*, he immediately realized a valuable lesson that still influences his writing:

> When you've got one or more people, okay two or more people, doing something that they know how to do, they're not going to talk about the thing that they're doing. Jules Winnfield and Vincent Vega were going to kill a guy, to terrorize him and kill him; well, I mean find out where the thing was that he had stolen and then terrorize him and then kill him. And on the way up to do that, they're talking about foot massages. That was a moment for me. I was like, holy crap, people—no matter who they are or what they're doing—need to talk just like regular people. And I think it was at that moment that I realized I shouldn't be looking at comic books as examples of how to write dialogue. I needed to be just listening to regular people in the real world. And that sort of clicked on the perpetual recording device in my head.

This movie-viewing experience is another example of a tool Micah has in his toolbox.

Thoughts of note. Micah shared his experiences generously, engaging with questions directly and commenting that his story might not apply to others. He acknowledged that writing is a skill that can be practiced and improved upon, but some innate abilities and a natural level of talent are still necessary for success. When asked about the need for skilled game writers, Micah said:

> A lot of the time, and I have enormous respect for level designers and game designers and programmers and whatnot, but they're not writers. And sometimes having a different perspective can help you head off a problem at an early enough stage that not a lot of work [that is eventually cut] gets done beforehand.

A seasoned freelancer, Micah's practical approach is an extension of the "pay the rent" motivation he had early in his career. That attitude, paired with drive, emotional intelligence, and skilled wordsmithing, has contributed to his success.

Conclusion. Micah's references to movie quotes and overhearing everyday speech as learning experiences serve as a reminder that learning happens in many settings. While some interviewees responded to questions about learning experience in terms of formal education, Micah was firm in his belief that lived experiences were just as important. He was also unique in his take on the roles of sensemaking and wordsmithing, presenting a casual attitude about simply doing the work asked of him. While he is a successful author outside of the game industry, Micah's responses echoed literature that framed game writing's purpose as enhancing other elements of the player experience (DeMarle, 2007; Sheldon, 2013). In highlighting the tensions that arise when the game's design cannot be reconciled with a reasonable story, even by the most skilled wordsmith and sensemaker, Micah offered an example of Skolnick's (2014) view that the professional game writer is best equipped to ensure the game story's success. For the other participants in this study, sensemaking requires more than clever wordsmithing.

"It's About Finding Balance."—Lou

Lou's responses brought new understanding to the role of the sensemaker by incorporating emotional intelligence in systems understanding, like the role of the advocate outlined by the other interviewees. Lou discussed the need for meaningful interaction with the members of other subdiscipline teams to achieve buy-in, while also demonstrating the need for self-assessment and confidence in championing ideas. Lou's focus on emotional intelligence, and past work experience outside of the game industry, differentiated this interview from others.

Lou has worked in the game industry for just under five years, working on a title experienced by over a million players. They continue to work as fiction writer. With a formal education in the liberal arts, Lou worked in the business world before entering the game industry. Lou was calm and reflective in our interview, and hesitant to say anything negative about their past experiences. They included recollections of discussions with their partner and other co-workers to help illustrate the connections between work life and personal life. Lou demonstrated energy and enthusiasm for the process of continually learning the craft in context.

Writing and storytelling. Lou referenced the basics of good writing several times throughout our interview and defined them as:

> An ability to write error-free prose with correct capitalization, punctuation, spelling, [and] sentence structure. A grasp of

connotation; the ability to write prose and dialogue that is evocative and clear and informative and that has voice. To write text that is flavorful and engaging; that shows a grasp of pacing.

We spent most of our interview discussing how game writing works beyond the writing basics, but it is important to share this clear-cut list of requirements for new writers. This detailed definition is valuable to aspiring game writers who may take traditional fundamentals for granted in a medium like games.

Lou was clear regarding the different skills required for writing, game writing, and narrative design. As our conversation evolved, Lou also discussed the overlap of these skills. They made a distinction between the game writer and the narrative designer as the person who crafts words for the game and the person who champions the story and decides how to implement it within the design team's vision, respectively. I asked if there was a distinction between the skills required of the two, and Lou responded:

> I could see where it might be acceptable for a narrative designer to be a little bit weaker on the basics of writing and character voice and dialogue. They would still need to understand story, and structure, and character, and what's important in those things and how you convey them. I could see where a writer could maybe get away with being a little less strong on the fundamentals of game design, as long as they had a narrative designer who could guide them very well. I think the more you have both roles good at both things, the better they're going to be at their jobs.

This response stood out from the other interviews. Many other interviewees referred to the narrative designer as a head game writer of sorts, seeing the distinction in terms of roles and responsibilities rather than skills. The other interviewees seemed to indicate that a narrative designer should have all the skills of a game writer, with the added responsibilities of advocating for story and communicating more formally with the other subdisciplines of the development team.

Lou was also clear about the distinction between the skills necessary for writers in other mediums and those working in games, though they did find some identical fundamentals. Lou said, "Being a good writer is about, in a lot of ways, being creative and being practiced at the mechanics. Being able to capture voice and intrigue and pacing; interesting world building." This goes for writers in any genre or medium.

Communication and collaboration. While discussing the distinctions between writing and game writing, Lou highlighted one major difference between their role as a novelist and their role in the game industry. Good game writers must also be advocates, Lou said:

> You have to learn how to be a good advocate for your ideas, which isn't the same as having good ideas. You have to learn what the other stakeholders around you want and how your proposals support or conflict with those goals. I think you have to learn how to manage relationships and personalities. How to present your ideas in a way that is constructive rather than assertive.

It is possible Lou developed these skills during their time working in the business world. Lou's reflective mindset and practice, together with emotional intelligence, have given them the skills necessary for making the often-difficult jump from creative writing to game writing.

In discussing the process of navigating studio dynamics and dealing with personalities in collaboration, Lou was explicit in their ability to "adjust communication strategies." I asked if this was the result of innate personality traits or professional experience. Lou indicated that emotional intelligence and effective communication could be learned:

> I do think it's something that anyone can learn with the right amount of focus and practice. Some people may be more naturally patient. Some people may be more naturally... collaborative, or consensus builders, but even if you're not those things by nature, I think when you understand *this* is the dynamic of *this* team, and *this* is how I need to operate within it, you can definitely learn it.

Lou was careful to point out that all teams are different, indicating that practicing agile interpersonal communication is an ongoing learning process.

When asked to discuss the collaborators Lou enjoyed working with most and least, the topic of communication styles surfaced again. Hesitant to mention anyone in a negative light, after a pause Lou remarked, "Well, there is one." Lou went on to discuss occasional tension with a member of another subdiscipline team, outlining their thoughts on what the possible underlying personal problems of this individual might be, in addition to clarifying the role the studio hierarchy played in the situation.

Lou reported that the individual in question had strong feelings regarding the game's story and often seemed defensive when collaborating. This individual had not been with the studio much longer than Lou, was in a "parallel place" in terms of hierarchy, and, perhaps more to the point, writing was not part of this person's official role. However, the individual still had ample opportunities to offer opinions in group meetings and in casual interactions with others on the team. Lou drew upon personal confidence and objectivity when approaching these tense scenarios:

> I have to adjust my communication strategies to try to approach them in the ways that they will be most receptive to. To be persistent and supportive and positive in those approaches. I guess I also to try and exercise the judgment between integrating their ideas and being respectful of [those ideas], but also not letting them push story or content in a way that does not fit our project.

Rather than using an approach that avoided confrontation or solely served to promote their own ideas strategically, Lou recognized the level of emotional investment others had in the project and made that a consideration.

In this sometimes-tense environment, Lou's approach seemed to go further than objectivity. Lou used the word "objectivity" several times throughout our interview; its usage seemed to indicate a quality of decision-making that avoids personal tastes. Rather than "choosing battles" and using judgment about what will ultimately, in Lou's opinion, be best for the game, Lou recognized that these moments of tension were also opportunities to build team cohesion and let others feel valued.

Understanding systems and dynamics. Lou discussed needing to understand the system of game development in terms of personal contributions and highlighted the need for confidence and a "certain degree of objectivity" in the collaborative process of game development. For good game writers, Lou said, this means:

> How to critique your own work not just in terms of, "Is this a good story, is this a good character?" but, like, "Does this play well with the systems that we're using? How can I make adjustments on my end to play better with the systems?" Or, "Are there any useful suggestions that I could make and make well for them to bring in an interesting story-related mechanic?"

For Lou, this means that the game writer must have confidence in their craft, their understanding of the game, and their ability to navigate the production system from the outset, producing the best work they can within the given constraints. This confidence, in Lou's view, leads to a capacity for objectivity that empowers the game writer to bring suggestions to the design team—not just suggestions to make, but suggestions to make well.

Lou noted that this ability to effectively advocate for story-related ideas is especially true when working on a role-playing game with a focus on story and character:

> A lot of people on the team have their own personal backgrounds—the RPGs they play and the things they like—and they don't like when some people have a very traditional aesthetic. Some people want to do something very offbeat and new. I think you do have to have enough confidence in your ideas to know when to champion them strongly, and when to listen and integrate and compromise.

A certain level of confidence is required for any creative writer, and, as a novelist, Lou has a sense of self-critique built into their own writing practices. When collaborating, objectivity regarding how well something works is gauged by one's personal level of confidence. Lou warned, "If you don't have some degree of confidence, you will always be Frankensteining your story into, or plastering a character into, what everyone else thinks it should be." Lou's term "Frankensteining" refers to a story that feels artificial and overwrought after too many additions and alterations by multiple team members, closer to Shelley's patchwork monster than something organic. The more confident Lou is in an idea and their ability to communicate that idea effectively, the more likely they are to advocate for it.

Tool proficiency. Lou and I discussed changes to portfolio content when transitioning from fiction to the game industry. Lou compiled a portfolio of short fiction pieces that matched the tone and style of what specific studios appeared to be looking for, even though these stories were not what Lou personally considered to be their best or most successful work. Lou had no interactive writing to present to employers but suggested that aspiring game writers should be able to demonstrate "a willingness to learn tools." Lou said:

> It might not be a bad idea to get some passing familiarity with a tool, just so you can demonstrate that and prove that you have some concept of what it means to script and set variables and check variables and all those things.

Understanding play. Lou referred to self-critique throughout the interview but also discussed the importance of analytical thinking when reading and playing games to become a better judge of what works. I asked if they could provide any exemplars of games with excellent writing or storytelling. Lou offered only a few, and referenced the games' critical reception rather than their personal assessment of them. Lou insisted on the importance of looking at successful games and analyzing what they did well. They also encouraged writers to ask, "Could this have been done better? Should this have been done differently?" Lou's focus on analyzing play indicated a need for understanding regarding play in the context of current trends in player tastes and critical reception.

Lou's associated learning experiences. Lou's transition from the business world to full-time fiction writer to writing for games was interesting, especially regarding how various skills and learning transferred from one professional arena to the next. When I asked Lou how they learned to successfully communicate and collaborate, they took a moment to think before responding, "I think I'm still learning it, honestly, and I try to pay a lot of attention to how my lead does these things. [...] That's someone who has more experience working with a lot of these personalities."

Lou also mentioned observation several times in our interview and described watching how others react in meetings and observing exchanges between team members. Lou's department lead's approach to compromise and managing conflict came to mind. Additionally, Lou mentioned asking for feedback not only on their writing but on their handling of situations. Lou explained that they sit down with members of other subdiscipline teams regularly so these team members can share their interests regarding the story.

Observation amplifies the benefits of reflective practice. Understanding the dynamics in the studio and gaining an appreciation for the personalities of all stakeholders organically takes time. Lou's observation speeds up that process by using co-workers as a resource. Lou acknowledged ties between their business background and their current role in the game industry, mentioning "all kinds of books on collaboration and stuff," but they also see value in reflective practice.

Thoughts of note. Lou's answers were nuanced. That nuance made the interview an engaging experience with much to draw from when analyzing my data collectively. Discussions of Lou's educational background led to many questions. While other interviewees made transitions from writer to game writer, Lou's experience came from what might seem to some like a different world entirely. As the discussion evolved, the overlap between the worlds of business and game development became apparent. Lou's formal education did not include game design, but a passion for writing, coupled with years of professional experience in the business world, served as strong preparation for a career in writing for games.

Conclusion. Like Micah, and perhaps explained by their shared pursuit of fiction writing outside the game industry, Lou stressed the value of crafting impactful stories. What set Lou's interview apart was their focus on understanding the systems of production while utilizing emotional intelligence during collaboration. This understanding of systems and recognition of their constant flux echoes key themes in both CHAT and RGS. Lou's careful attention to systems when making judgment calls regarding when to advocate for an idea and when to relent aligns with the thinking of CHAT scholars like Engeström (1999) and Foot (2014), who saw the value in identifying tensions and contradictions within systems as illuminating areas for possible innovation. Lou's approach aligns with Schön's (2017) model of the reflective practitioner—another important resource for consideration in developing game writing pedagogy.

"It's All Different Thinking"—Peter

Peter's responses focused on systems and tools. He shared thoughts exemplifying the sensemaker and advocate roles by highlighting the need for communication across teams in many different forms to ensure the success of a game's story. He stressed that all members of the development team play a part in telling the game's story, and that knowledge of storytelling principles should be shared by all subdisciplines. While other participants referenced tools in terms of aptitude in self-teaching, Peter was explicit regarding the need for game writers to be able to master and manipulate tools to meet the needs of the project.

Peter has worked in the game industry for 16 years, working on nearly 50 titles experienced by over 100 million players. He also writes comics and non-fiction. His formal education was at a large, four-year state university that offered an individualized study degree. Peter's program of study involved components of writing and visual design. Peter worked in comics before his career in games. While allowing for exceptions, most of Peter's answers were exact. This degree of clarity was likely due to his extensive industry experience; it allowed us to specifically examine several areas of interest.

Peter and I had met at several conferences before the interview, and we had discussed the merits of films related to their applicability to game writing instruction. In social settings, I try to avoid questions such as "What are the functional competencies required for game writers?" and instead cover topics such as "Should I make my students watch *The Godfather*?" Peter and most others in the game writing community, in my experience, are almost always interested in these types of conversations. I asked Peter to describe the differences between writing individually and working in the game studio environment. He was quick to respond, "It's all different thinking," followed by an emphatic pause (punctuated with some intense eye contact).

Writing and storytelling. Many of the interviewees stressed the differences between game writing and traditional creative writing. Peter did this as well, but he was especially interested in discussing how other subdisciplines play a part in telling the game's story. Peter was a strong advocate for the incorporation of a narrative designer who champions narrative throughout the development process while interfacing and coordinating with the game writing team. Rather than just game writers, Peter shared that all members of the development team need to know the fundamentals of storytelling. He explained:

> They have to have some idea of what to do. On their own, at their desk. And so, if they've got a good grounding in narrative principles, established, known narrative principles—the same ones that I'm working under when I create the idea for the story, or I give them ideas for the story—then they're going to make better decisions.

Peter's sentiment might seem obvious, but the low importance placed on writing in the industry means this knowledge is often overlooked. If all members of the development team possessed this storytelling knowledge, as Peter suggested, the game's story would reach its full potential.

Peter noted seeing an increased awareness of narrative principles, such as Joseph Campbell's monomyth from *The Hero with a Thousand Faces* (1972) and the basics of the three-act structure, in the game design community. He found this increased awareness encouraging for the future of storytelling in the medium but noted the lack of a firm foundation. According to Peter, the passing familiarity one might gain from YouTube videos or Wikipedia articles is not enough to fully and actively engage those narrative principles.

Communication and collaboration. For game writers, learning the lexicon of the other subdisciplines in the studio is important for communication, sensemaking, and helping achieve buy-in from others involved in the production. Peter shared, "What I've learned is that the team tells the story, not the game writer. Game development is a team effort. And narrative is one part of that team effort." He stated that, at this point in his career, his focus has widened to encompass not only game writing but also educating the entire development team about storytelling. He explained:

> I can write down the idea for a mission, or a fantastic cutscene script, or a cool scripted event. But in the end, the moment-to-moment execution of all the things the player sees and experiences while playing through that mission, that part of the story, will be created by other people. They may or may not have any idea what the main story is that they're contributing to. They may not have any idea whether the decisions they're making are actually going to affect the storytelling.

Peter's statement highlighted the challenge of incorporating a cohesive story into a game created by hundreds of individuals.

Creating a game with a successful narrative requires communication between teams. This relates to Peter's sentiment that everyone involved in development must have a solid foundation in storytelling principles. Members of the writing team must be experts, but the contributions of all subdiscipline teams are "going to help the storytelling, or negatively impact the storytelling," so teaching those storytelling principles to everyone is important.

Understanding systems and dynamics. Understanding the writing affordances of different game genres and platforms is vital to applying creative writing skills to game writing. Combined with the player's expectation of interactivity, these constraints constitute one major difference between writing for games and other mediums or in other settings.

I pressed Peter to describe the similarities between his process working alone and his collaborative process in writing for games. I asked if the "actual writing of words on the page" was the same; his response was a simple, "Nope." He then continued:

> It's all different thinking because you may be writing for a very big-stage AAA console title on one assignment, where you're able to write three-minute cutscenes and have a conversation system, and have branching dialogue and a branching story, and scripted events happening in the mission. And you might have systemic dialogue with tens of thousands of lines to support combat. Or, you

might have almost none of those things. You might have only little portrait pop-ups with text dialogue for a mobile title.

Peter began his career in games as a producer, so he was familiar with the development process before he took on game writing roles. The academic literature mentioned the lack of a unified format in game writing but proposed that standardized practices might evolve over time (Stoddard, 2016). Peter disagreed with this notion, citing the continually changing technology and organizational structures of game development. The link between these views and the theoretical framework of this study are mentioned in the conclusion of this section.

Tool proficiency. Peter discussed the necessity of using and manipulating common tools, such as Microsoft Excel, to suit the purposes of game writing. He noted that Excel is often used in the industry, even though other, game-specific software now exists. Peter stressed the importance of mastering tools one can modify and manipulate to suit the needs of a project. This speaks to the lack of a standard format for game scripts.

The given format for a specific project is dictated by the nature of the gameplay, the process of development, and the preferences of those involved in making the game. Peter explained:

> You figure it out, because that's what we're often faced with is solving those problems and how to organize information and track information. And hand something off to your junior writers that they can understand too, that they can work from.

Good writing and mastering storytelling principles are minimum requirements for game writers. The ability to adapt those skills in multiple forms is a key difference between game writing and writing in other narrative genres.

Understanding play. According to Peter, mastering narrative principles allows game writers to spend less energy telling a story and more energy making it work with the gameplay. In his view, game writers should be thinking about the following:

> What verbs does a player use when playing the game? That will define who you are and probably what kind of conflict have you found to solve. Probably the one thing I'd say is in common to all those things is really understanding that you're not writing for any other medium than for a game. And that you need to be thinking

in terms of gameplay verbs and mechanics and how your story can enhance them and contextualize them.

Peter explained that he continues to play a lot of games. Creating an experience for the player requires adopting their mindset and trying to figure out how they will interact with the world and scenarios presented to them. He mentioned needing knowledge of a game to truly understand and meaningfully contribute to it. Some of Peter's play is in the name of research, as he seeks to understand trends in the market for a new project or gain familiarity with the titles connected with a specific studio.

Peter's associated learning experiences. My interview with Peter evolved differently from the others and did not include any discussion about his educational background. I clarified to all interviewees that "learning experiences" could be anything, so he may not have seen his formal education as vital to the discussion. When asked what he attributed his success to, he offered, "I understand how traditional stories are made; I understand how games are made because I've managed the execution of many of them. Now I can combine these two careers into one."

Thoughts of note. Peter drew on his long and varied experience in the game industry to answer questions and offer advice. At one point he said, "Depending on your hard drive space, we may get into all that," referring to some of the topics we did not have a chance to cover during our interview. He kindly offered to assist in any further studies, and we have informally discussed these topics off the record.

Conclusion. Peter insisted that game writers must understand the systems and related tools used in the industry. Rather than focusing on creative invention, as highlighted in some of the previous interviews, Peter noted the importance of all subdisciplines in telling the game's story—an important note to consider for the CGD programs training future game industry employees. Peter's response is evocative of Paul Prior's (2003) conception of writing as a process that takes place in a structure of participation, and his statement that "tracing [that process] involves examining who is involved in making the text and in what ways" (p. 170). The prior knowledge of the industry Peter cites as a learning experience is akin to genre knowledge and understanding the activity system of production. Though Peter did not directly utilize those terms, his analysis seemed to call for those theoretical lenses in developing an effective pedagogy of game writing, and perhaps an effective approach to curriculum design in CGD.

"You're the Wrapper."—Garreth

Garreth's responses centered around appreciating the individuals involved in the system of production. His passion for the advocate role, which he termed "evangelist," and wordsmithing demonstrated the need to share one's own skill and enthusiasm to inspire others. He also provided insight regarding the role of the story and the game writer's work in the player experience. While Garreth's passion for storytelling aligned with Micah's and Lou's, the realities of production tempered it. He offered further insight regarding the systems of production, stressing the perceptions and well-being of those affected by creative decisions.

Garreth has worked in the game industry for 14 years, working on five major titles experienced by over 16 million players. He also writes screenplays. Garreth began his first studio job soon after he graduated from college. His formal education is a degree in theater from a four-year state university. Throughout our interview, Garreth recalled his educational experiences in detail and expressed the value of his college experience. Garreth's responses were candid and colorful.

Writing and storytelling. While he identifies as a writer and loves story in games, Garreth acknowledged that the context game writers provide is an additive to the core experience: "It's a cherry on top." He acknowledged that many of the narrative-focused elements of games, such as cinematic cutscenes, are ignored by players wanting to continue play:

> I'm a writer. I love writing. I'm a voice director. I love voices. Do you know how many games I play where they're totally muted? Like, "Oh man, my kid's sitting next to me." It's not disrespect for the craft; it's a thing that I can't go and listen to right now.

In this regard, it bears mentioning that most game writers I have interacted with agree that players should be able to skip through these cinematic elements, believing that the game's story should be present without relying on writing to explain it. Telling the story through gameplay is the challenge, which is one of the reasons why communicating with others on the development team is so vital.

Garreth's feelings on managing the expectations of others in the role of the game writer played into his thoughts on egotism in writers. Truly understanding and embracing the role of the game writer is vital to thriving in the studio environment, but with experience and confidence in one's abilities, it is easy to forget the role that game writing plays in the overall development process. He warned aspiring game writers:

> It's not about the story you want to tell. It's about the game you want someone to experience. The game is so much more than the story. The game is how the user picks up the things, how they feel as they're attacking [...] It's so amazing and it's so powerful, but it's powerful and it's amazing because you trust other people to do their job too.

Just as the game writer must work within the limitations of the form and write what is demanded of them, others in the studio have similar challenges. All individual contributions to a game are subject to the restrictions of time, technology, or creative decision-making.

Garreth also made a clear contrast to writing fiction, or for the stage and screen, noting that video games are a collaborative commercial enterprise: "It's a job. It's a business. You're a commercial artist, not an auteur. [...] Go do your own thing on your own time." He stressed that game writing is an artistic collaboration undertaken by a team of individuals, warning that "[t]he moment that you start sacrificing the game for you wanting to tell a story, you're in the wrong business." Even though they must focus on the work they have been commissioned to make, collaborating with many others and making compromises along the way, the process of game writers is still very much an artistic pursuit.

An interjection for this book: I checked in with participants after data analysis and let them take a look at any quotations I planned on using. This was a last check on anonymity—a few folks asked for changed pronouns but no other flags were raised—and a chance for participants to weigh in regarding their portrayal. Even as identities were protected, Garreth took some exceptions with how he might come across to readers. Revisiting our interview, and reflecting on interactions with Garreth, I feel the need to reinforce his support for aspiring game writers and developers. This participant did not hold back; he embraced the context and was forthcoming. The fact that Garreth worried, months after the fact, that he may sound discouraging to aspiring writers is a testament to how supportive the game writing community is.

Being flexible in completing writing tasks as assigned was mentioned by most of the interviewees, but Garreth said that the goal should be to present decision-makers with options. A game writer must have the ability to produce bespoke work, but a skilled writer should be able to conceive of multiple options for each prompt, like considering multiple pathways for players to follow. We discussed a hypothetical scenario where designers decided the game needed zombies in level three. Garreth said that the writer's job is not to simply make these zombies "make sense" through writing, but to give multiple options that make the zombies' inclusion "cool" so the designers have a range of options equally effective in telling the game's story. The writer, Garreth said, "shouldn't be subservient, but it's about understanding what people are asking for and then using your craft to interpret what they want and then delivering that to a high level."

Garreth's presentation of this hypothetical scenario included the same colorful language and strong sentiments of "get over yourself" presented at other points in our interview, but his tone was positive and indicated a real passion for his craft. Garreth seemed to view the skill of presenting options as a method for expressing creativity and enhancing the game. He said, "It's your job to make [the game] cool," rather than just providing context to have it make sense. In this way, the flexible and efficient game writer can enhance the player's overall experience. Even though the writer may not control the overall direction of the game's story, they can provide content that is visible in the final product.

Communication and collaboration. Garreth spoke of communication and collaboration in terms of his co-workers' reactions to given situations. Beyond the basic communication skills required to work effectively, Garreth expressed the need to engage further and try to understand what matters to fellow collaborators. He mentioned the need to find out "what's important to them" in the game. Garreth framed this competency as a characteristic, a trait that some possess more than others. He acknowledged that writing fundamentals and communication are important, but also offered:

> The other half of it, and the psychological part of it, is I do believe that there are certain personality types that are not cut out to be writers in the games industry. I really do believe that. That's a [sh***y] thing to say, but I think it's totally true.

Switching gears to address the question from the perspective offered by having a leadership role—one that he occupied at the time of our interview—Garreth explained the importance of empathy in the studio:

> Anything that you're asking your team, those people, to go and do because you think it's really, really neato is costing someone time. They'll never get that time back. So, you writing some [f***ing] crazy wide shot with 100 people running, charging up the gate or whatever, requires you to ask, "Is that [sh*t] really more important than someone getting to spend time with their family on Thanksgiving?"

Sometimes the answer is yes, Garreth said, because his confidence in an idea and his judgment regarding its value to the project makes it necessary. He explained that if the answer is yes, then he must sell the idea to others and engage in the work directly.

Beyond appreciating the work of those in other subdisciplines, Garreth expressed a need to get a sense of what things are important, generally, to people in those subdisciplines, and to appreciate the beliefs and aesthetics common among that specific group. Having an appreciation of these processes and beliefs allows for deeper communication, which is an important step to truly understanding the individuals on any team.

Understanding systems and dynamics. Successful game writers give context to all the moving parts that make up a player's experience. This requires, as other interviewees have mentioned, understanding the work of, and communicating with, other subdisciplines. Rather than viewing game writing as sensemaking, Garreth chose the term "evangelizing." According to him, "You're there to be the thin layer of glue that connects multiple disciplines and offers motivation for the player."

He highlighted the need for the game writers to serve as champions for the story and to get others in the development team interested. This same strategy of evangelizing is also applied to out-of-game writing tasks, such as marketing or generating enthusiasm for a new title in the player community. I asked Garreth how he felt about these out-of-game writing tasks and he responded enthusiastically:

> The writer, it's a natural bridge, because, generally speaking, the writer is a cheerleader for the product and is also the person... he is, or I guess I should say they are, but I'm referring to my experience... the writer is the bridge between gameplay and narrative, right? You have to be able to go and.... You're the wrapper around

all these different elements of the game. It's important to go and be familiar with the art, be familiar with the game design. You walk between these worlds, so you can go and act as the bridge between these things.

Facilitating communication between the subdisciplines and driving a unified vision of the game's story translates to communication outside of the studio in the form of marketing, public speaking, and other interactions with players and potential players. It stands to reason that these same skills might allow someone to assume lead producer and lead designer roles within a studio, as producing and designing involve generating enthusiasm and building a sense of community within a high-stress work environment.

Tool proficiency. Garreth's interview focused primarily on the higher-order thinking skills required for creativity and collaboration. He was able to learn the tools of the trade on the job but noted that aspiring game writers must learn game development software as free-to-use game engines become more common, and competition for jobs increases. In Garreth's view, writers who can use these tools have an advantage, as they can demonstrate their skills: "Download this [video game level editor tool] and now, all of a sudden, you have my entire mod of, 'Here's my stuff. You can see what it looks like.' It's totally different now."

He noted that tool proficiency is vital for college students studying to be in the game industry. Demonstrating familiarity with engines and scripting "shows that you learn things and fail things. It's not theoretical; it's a practice." This allows students to capitalize on the education gained through their college experience.

Understanding play. *Dungeons and Dragons* (*D&D*) helped Garreth develop a sense of who players are and what they want through play. Though he reported that current work and family life commitments limit the time available for following this pursuit, Garreth is a longtime, avid player of *D&D*. He illustrated the importance of play by sharing a story from his high school days. Some close friends from his usual *D&D* group moved away, so Garreth found a new group of players. *D&D* is a game that can be played in very different ways, Garreth explained, and he took for granted that his original group was approaching it the right way. After initial frustration and disappointment, Garreth realized that *D&D* could be experienced any number of ways, equally enjoyable, depending on each group or player's preferences. It was a valuable learning experience.

This experience of play revealed to Garreth how tension could arise in any collaborative activity. He felt frustrated when he found it difficult to adapt to the new group, but later realized that "every one of those people can say, 'I love *D&D*.' But what does that mean? How do you love *D&D*? Why do you love *D&D*?'" In hindsight, he also learned about managing others' expectations and accounting for the multitude of ways players can enjoy a game. Two players may have separate views of what *D&D* should look like, he realized, and "neither of those players is wrong."

Garreth's associated learning experiences. Garreth's educational background is in theater, and he was eager to share his college experiences. As he referenced specific course numbers and curriculum specifics, the experiences seemed fresh in his mind. He also shared some opinions on current CGD programs. Looking back on his education after 14 years of industry experience, he noted that his study of theater provided valuable preparation for his current work. At first, he mentioned a specific CGD program he felt was doing a good job preparing students, but later explained the most vital factor in finding industry employment:

> Portfolio wins. Portfolio always wins. It's that [good] schools give you more opportunity to go and create portfolio pieces. It's what I was talking about, the same thing about a safe place to fail. It's not about them. [X University's] not a better education than any other place. I think my [theater] education at [Y University] was a better preparation for the games industry than some of the people that I see.

A major benefit of Garreth's college experience was learning collaborative practice through theater. He saw the relevance of his theater background early in his career, realizing, "It's the same stuff. It's just different. Instead of a set designer, an actor, [a] lighting designer, and product manager, it's design, programming, art."

Though his focus at school was on playwriting, he recalled, "I literally had a course called 'Collaboration in the Arts.'" His degree program required writers to work directly with set designers and actors to get a sense of their work and processes. He considered the lessons he learned through that collaborative coursework directly applicable to his game industry experience.

Garreth shared his perception that many writers do not value college, finding that most courses have little applicability to their craft. Responding to those who doubt the value of a college education, Garreth said:

> I disagree with that, not because I believe that you learn something amazing in college and it's kept secret if you don't complete

your degree. The most important thing that you get out of college, if the student's willing to take it [...] is the ability to safely fail. It's the ability to experiment and try something and let it be a total [g****mn] mess and there's no stakes involved because it's not your family, it's not your job. It's a grade.

More than once, Garreth emphasized the term "higher learning," showing his understanding that the educational experience is about more than receiving a degree.

Thoughts of note. While he might have been prepared to share advice for students as he has done in talks and interviews before, Garreth seized the chance to explore his experiences. Returning to my research questions toward the end of the interview, I asked Garreth about the skills, abilities, knowledge, and characteristics he looks for in game writers. He replied bluntly, "The most important characteristic is don't be an [a**hole]." He continued:

I cannot stress that enough. It is the most important thing. It is the most important thing because you spend so much time working with these people. You're there late nights. You're... The people that you work with become a surrogate family. You build relationships with these people. If you don't want to spend time, if you don't want to go be in the trenches with this person for 80 hours, [f*ck] off.

Garreth is a writer with strong opinions, passions, and energy. He seemed happy to help aspiring game writers and college students interested in the game industry.

Conclusion. Garreth presented a behind-the-scenes look at what it means to be a game writer and what it means to manage writers. He demonstrated the importance of understanding systems and emotional intelligence—having a level of empathy for others when considering the constraints of working in the system of production. Using roughly the same language as Margaret, Garreth stressed the need for a basic level of collegiality in game writers. When viewed through the lenses of CHAT and RGS, this quality is a conceptual tool rather than merely a desirable personality trait. Additionally, Garreth's inclusion of the role of narrative elements in the player experience echoed the literature that situates game writing as gripping yet disposable, ultimately serving the other elements of the game (Sheldon, 2013; Skolnick, 2014; Stoddard, 2016). This reality is complicated by the knowledge that game writers work in a context where financial concerns often drive creative decisions (Tschang, 2007). Consequently, the result of some tasks might not be appreciated, or even experienced, by some players.

"How Long Is a Piece of String?"—Henry

Henry's responses centered on the role of wordsmithing and how it fits within game production. His response regarding the thrill inherent in writing a good line of dialogue captured the essence of the word-smith role. Henry also shared his experiences as an advocate outside the studio, constantly championing the importance and economic efficiency of good storytelling in games. This led to some discussion of the historical factors that affect game writing and the medium of games. A freelancer like Micah, Henry embraces the challenges of game writing that other writers may seem as limiting creativity.

Henry's careful distinction between creation and execution, comparison to other art forms, and framing the medium in historical context set this interview apart.

Henry has worked in the game industry for ten years, working on 14 titles experienced by over 100 million players. Henry also simultaneously continues a successful career as a comic writer. He was a graphic design major in college. I met Henry during a conference. I spoke with him and attended one of his talks, and he shared resources for use in my classroom. The interview was conducted over Skype.

I began our interview by asking Henry to explain what a game writer does. He responded, "Well, how long is a piece of string?" implying that this is a difficult, or perhaps impossible, question to answer out of context. Game writing is complex, and it varies significantly in different settings.

Henry generously shared details about his past experiences and career path, noting that he had worked in other fields before settling on writing comics and, eventually, game writing. We talked about the unique aspects of writing in the game industry, how it relates to film and comics, and how skilled game writers will play a role in the evolution and ultimate sophistication of video games as a medium.

Writing and storytelling. According to Henry, one of the keys to good writing comes through self-assessment and criticism. He felt that writing was unique from other art forms in this sense, saying, "If I pick up a pen and paper and start to do a drawing, I can tell very quickly whether or not I am a good artist. Same with a paintbrush. Same with a 3D graphics program." Those mediums, Harry said, allow for an immediate assessment of quality, whereas writing requires a deeper level of critique. He said:

I think a good writer with a good critical faculty will know when something isn't working. I think we're all very good at fooling ourselves, but at the same time, we know in the back of our minds when we've written something that isn't all that great. Not always, but I think, generally, that's…. If you're halfway through writing something, and you're just not feeling it, and there's nothing about it that's exciting you, then maybe this project isn't going to work.

Interestingly, Henry retracted his comment that writing was unique in this regard, mentioning that photography falls in the same category. The act of putting words down on a page and deciding if the work is good was likened to taking a photograph and being satisfied in the same way. Self-perception of skill level can easily mislead an aspiring writer or photographer, so seeking feedback from others is a vital part of development.

Henry clearly outlined the competencies required for success in game writing, though his answer was framed with skepticism regarding the need for skills specific to games. He also seemed to question his own definition of skills, but shared:

You need to be able to tell a story, obviously. You need to be able to know how stories are constructed, how they're put together, how characters work. You need to be able to write good dialogue and all that sort of thing. I'm not saying that those aren't genuine skills. Of course, they are, but they're…. If you're doing creative writing of any kind, you need to have those skills.

Later in the interview, Henry discussed his hesitance to define these items as skills generally, noting that they are difficult to teach and demonstrate to others.

Communication and collaboration. Henry reported that, in much of his game writing experience, he was brought onto the team after production was already underway. This scenario is common in the industry. Though attitudes are slowly changing, the perception is that a writer is not needed until most of the game's assets are developed. A writer is then added to the team to perform the writing tasks required for providing content and context.

Henry discussed some scenarios where he was hired very late in the development process—out of necessity—to fix the game's narrative. Detailing one of these scenarios, Henry discussed the importance of understanding the rationale behind others' creative decisions. When brought onto a project, he asks questions such as "So, why are you doing this?" and gauges the responses in hopes of creating work that aligns with the original intent as closely as possible.

In some cases, though, games have fundamental issues that even the most skilled wordsmith cannot fix. The same communication skills that aid Henry in game writing are sometimes called upon for actual design work. He explained:

> There have been cases where I've come in later on a game and have had to salvage, for want of a better word, something that might have a, should we say, not fully realized narrative design. And so even though I've been brought in late, I've had to, by necessity of writing the script, I've had to actually go in and redesign parts of the narrative and work with the producers and the game director and stuff to actually say, "Okay, we need to actually make some changes here. Not just to the words I'm writing, but to the way this is implemented, the way we present it to the player, and, in fact, the direction that the story will take."

Again, the sensemaking a writer brings to the process of making a game has its limits. Attempting to understand the intent of the designers allows the game writer to make useful suggestions that align with the game's original vision. The scenario Henry mentions above was only applied after he made every attempt to make the original vision work.

Understanding systems and dynamics. Beyond the ability to write well, Henry highlighted how game writers must understand the functions of a studio. While all studios differ in their practices, writers with some knowledge of common tasks and the roles they play in the system of development are highly valuable to the industry. In terms of in-studio writing tasks, Henry made an early distinction between creation and execution. For him, creation involves any process of coming up with and refining ideas. Execution is applying one's craft to bring that creation to fruition. He mentioned that writers focused on crafting words, rather than on creating stories, are likely to thrive in game writing. He said:

> If you are the sort of writer who writes a line of dialogue that is just absolutely perfect for a particular character, and for that time and that scene, and then you can sit back and reread it and go, "Woah, yeah," and get a good feeling out of that, then you actually will be quite well-suited to games writing, because a lot of games writing, unless you're at that producer level, is like that.

According to Henry, embracing craftsmanship is the way to overcome the perceived loss of creative control some game writers report. He said, "The control you have is to execute your craft, use your skills, and write great, perfect little lines of dialogue here and there. That's the thrill that you're going to get out of it."

Like several other interviewees, Henry suggested alternative vocations for those who do not find satisfaction in the kind of work required for game writing. Of the bespoke writing common in the game studio, he said:

> If you don't get a thrill from that, then maybe game writing isn't for you. Maybe you should go into screenwriting or TV writing or something. But if you are craft-focused in that way and you're willing to, for at least for a while in your career anyway, be an executor rather than a sort of big decisionmaker, then games writing can actually be.... Yes, it's stressful, but it can actually be quite fulfilling.

Henry discussed the limitations placed on game writers as problems to be solved. At no point in our interview did he lament any lack of creative control.

Tool proficiency. Henry mentioned the importance of making and playing games to learn about interactivity and how narrative functions in interactive spaces, but said he continues to make "little narrative indie games" on his own, to experiment. Using basic free-to-use tools, he explored things he might not have a chance to explore in a professional setting. He mentioned that demonstrating ideas through relevant tools allows him to communicate ideas more clearly with designers. Although rudimentary in terms of audiovisual execution, as the games created this way are primarily clickable text, Henry noted how simple games can convey ideas beyond a pitch. These games can help people envision potential and increase the likelihood of ideas being implemented or adopted by the development team.

Understanding play. One major hurdle skilled writers face when trying to write for games is understanding interactivity and play. Henry commented that the appreciation for a writer who understands games and interactivity has only become apparent to the industry in the last five to seven years. "Prior to that," he noted, "it was very, very common, and it still does happen, that developers would call up their favorite Hollywood screenwriter or TV writer or somebody and say, 'Can you go and write a script for a game?'"

In Henry's view, writing for games is a "much more esoteric skill, because that's the sort of thing you only get from playing a lot of games."

He discussed the rise of the professional game writer that has resulted from the years of "predictably variable" results when bringing in writers from other mediums. He said:

> [...] Whereas now developers have realized, and because there has been this rise of the professional writer within games, thank goodness, developers have started to realize that, actually, having a writer who understands games, who plays games, who knows how games work, who understands the way games are constructed, who understands the way they're developed, who literally understands what happens inside a game studio, that's actually an important part of being a game writer, even though it's not creative, in a sense.

Having the knowledge Henry outlined above makes the writer more effective in the studio. That knowledge is what makes him or her a successful game writer.

Likely, the establishment of the professional game writer role has arisen from two factors. The first is sales and critical reception: games with strong stories and skilled writing are among the most successful in the current market. The second is related to stories like Henry's, where the writer is brought on too late and the studio realizes how valuable his or her contribution would have been throughout the entire process.

Henry's associated learning experiences. Henry enthusiastically recalled an experience from his high school days, and a teacher who "took a bunch of us, you know, sort of, yeah, blue-collar, working-class kids, and showed us how to appreciate and love Shakespeare, and thank goodness for that." Henry credited this course with igniting his passion for stories of all kinds, giving him a deeper appreciation for the comics and novels he already knew. He remains a voracious reader.

Building confidence in his craft was another important learning experience for Henry. He mentioned, "You won't find a writer alive that isn't slightly insecure about their writing." He continues to build these skills by learning through collaboration. He said:

> It's very difficult to tell whether or not what you've written is very good until you give it to other people, [...] to show your final work and say, "I think this is all right. How about you?" That takes quite a bit of self-confidence and a certain amount of, well, either bravery or naiveté. Take your pick.

Taking risks in pursuing creative careers before his transition to the games industry helped Henry build that confidence.

According to Henry, making games is vital to learning the craft of game writing. He said, "Just making some kind of game through to completion is so much more instructive than any amount of theory or listening to people like me ramble on." He noted sharing this advice regularly when approached by aspiring game writers

Thoughts of note. Henry expressed optimism for the future of game writing; he believes the evolution of storytelling in games is inevitable. He shared that game narrative is "really, really cheap" compared to the resources and compensation that go into other parts of the game. The industry can no longer deny the value of quality game writing because that writing has an enormous impact on the player's experience and, in most cases, the game's financial and critical success. At the very least, he said, no one has ever played a game and said, "Oh, but the story's too good."

Henry asserted that writers' passion for stories is not unique, but a shared human experience: "People love great stories." When discussing the abilities or characteristics of the writer, Henry, though hesitantly, mentioned the need for a level of innate talent:

> To an extent, I think that is true. If you are—I don't want to say born to be a writer because that implies sort of selection of some kind, and I'm very much a believer in you make your own destiny, and you make your own luck and take advantage of the opportunities that hard work brings you.

Margaret and, in the following section, Robert shared this sentiment and stated it explicitly. In all three cases, the interviewees acknowledged that while there is no set path to a career as a game writer, hard work and taking advantage of opportunities are vital.

Conclusion. Henry highlighted two major difficulties for writers entering the game industry: failure to embrace writing as execution rather than creation, and failure to understand the importance of play and interactivity. Valuing self-assessment was echoed in other interviews, but Henry's comparison of game writing to other art forms was noteworthy given the disparate subdisciplines involved in game production. The basic quality of a line of code or animation sequence is apparent through its ability to function. Making the same judgment for writing requires more nuance. Henry's voluntary inclusion of historical context situated the game writer within the systems of game production and game culture. His call for a study of the day-to-day workings of game writers echoed Bazerman and Prior's (2004) call to explore the practices of writing in context and how those practices gain meaning or function as dynamic elements within specific cultural settings. Incorporating that context suggests the benefits RGS might have for industry practice and for the medium.

"Logic Matters. Doing Math Matters."—Robert

Robert's responses revolved around the game writer's ability to work within systems as a sensemaker and wordsmith. He said, "Logic matters. Doing math matters." Throughout the interview, he also stressed that game writers must work quickly and communicate effectively. Robert's focus on systems echoed the way the other participants presented them as a unique challenge for writers within game production, but Robert framed the individual's role as navigation rather than negotiation. After stating simply, "to be a good game writer you have to be a good writer," Robert's responses focused on game-industry-specific tasks. In addition to describing the value he found in a liberal arts education, Robert stressed different forms of self-learning as vital to success for game writers.

Robert has worked in the game industry for eight years, working on several titles experienced by over 100 million players. He also writes plays and screenplays. His formal education was a degree in psychology with a minor in philosophy from a four-year liberal arts college. He also obtained post-graduate degrees in theater and creative writing.

My interviews with Robert took place at two conferences, separated by ten months. I first met Robert three years prior to our interview. He always seemed keen to hear about my teaching experiences and was eager to share his thoughts on his process and professional experiences.

Writing and storytelling. Robert framed the role of the game writer in terms of industry perception, discussing the attributes companies look for in hiring: "[Studios] want people who are going to be dedicated to actually doing the job. They get concerned with novelists, and I feel that way sometimes too, you know?" Robert explained that some writers feel a lengthy process is necessary for good work, admitting that he once believed the same, so the speed and flexibility required of game writers might feel unnatural to those new to the industry. He said:

> Writing is very often a solitary activity, right? You're kind of alone with your thoughts. Being in a studio, you're almost never completely alone. It's usually an open-office scenario; people can

interrupt each other at any time. A lot of times, people will put on headphones, music, listen, zone out. In some ways, it's a skill, because you have to learn to navigate your day and being in an office in a place where you've got to be creative, and you got to find your own time.

Given the many interworking teams and assets involved in game production, the context this writing takes place within is a major part of defining the game writer's work.

According to Robert, the game writer exists to bridge the gap between gameplay and story. He explained that the game writer's focus should be on enhancing the story rather than creating it, by adding context for the player via text and dialogue based on the given game design elements. I asked about the skills required for the job, and he responded:

I think as a game writer you have to be a good writer, period, first, right? All the basics. Understanding story, character, plot, diction, all this stuff about storytelling and word choice, and I think for game writing, brevity is much more important, even than in other media.

Later in the interview, Robert discussed the need for speed and efficiency in game writing, saying simply, "Game writers need to be fast."

This need for speed was best illustrated when Robert described other game writers he admired. When asked to describe the best game writer he had worked with, after a brief pause followed by visible enthusiasm Robert said:

Oh, man. Okay. There're two people that come to mind immediately, one of whom I've worked with, one of whom I haven't really worked with, but I've seen their samples, and I understand a lot about how they work. They are fast. Extremely fast. They are organized and anal, and yet their delivered work is compelling and stunning despite how fast it is, right? You know, it's like someone that's fast, usually if you're really fast you're turning in something that's a little subpar. If you're turning in something that's amazing, it's usually a little slower, right?

It is interesting that Robert felt compelled to include someone he has never worked with in his response. This could indicate the high value placed on the skills of writing well and efficiently. It could also indicate that the uniquely and remarkably high skill level this individual possesses is worthy of discussion within the game writing community.

Robert highlighted the importance of revision and editing in game writing but presented those skills as distinct from writing. This surprised me, given Robert's thoughts on self-critique. In a process that often looks like, "You have this much dialogue to write in this much time [...] Get it done. Be done. And turn it around," specializing roles and associated tasks aids efficiency. According to Robert, tasking editing and revision to individuals not directly involved in the creation of the in-game text allows for rapider iteration.

Communication and collaboration. As noted in the literature and by most of this study's participants, all the elements of the player experience are part of telling the story. Learning to communicate clearly with other subdiscipline teams allows game writers to get a sense of what is possible in terms of content and function. Robert explained:

> In the field, you have to work with people, and it is really hard. You have to really... like I was describing earlier, you have to be very adaptive. You have to be able to communicate across disciplines, which sometimes is not easy for writers to do. [...] If I can discuss things the way that a programmer might discuss a mechanical system, that gives me a leg up [as a writer] because I can express why my story is going to be good in the programming that he's writing, or she's writing.

Game writers can make better storytelling decisions with this knowledge, possibly incorporating the story ideas of all members of the development team. Robert continued:

> Same way with designers. I can talk to a designer; I can talk to an artist. If I can talk in a visual language, I'm going to accomplish more on a team to get my vision through. If I'm bad at that, they aren't going to care, and they aren't going to want to work with me and make this work because they'll just kind of dismiss it.

Effective communication allows for greater creative freedom, in Robert's view, and gives a game writer a greater sense of authorship in the game.

Robert also discussed managing expectations and priorities when collaborating. He referred to this skill as having the self-discipline necessary for balancing the priorities of completing one's own tasks with other obligations, such as attending meetings. Making the distinction between this skill in creative writing and game writing, he said, "If you're home and you're disciplined, that just means you have self-discipline. But if you're at the office and you have discipline, it means that you know how to navigate the daily distractions." Robert further explained how productive collaboration in the hectic studio environment requires more than just communicating and managing personalities.

Understanding systems and dynamics. The distinction between creative writing and game writing was a theme that surfaced naturally during the interview. Part of the distinction highlighted game writing's role within the larger system of game development. When asked, "What are the necessary skills a game writer must possess?" he responded:

> Yeah, so to me there's different skillsets. There is the talent, right? The ability to develop characters and stories and ideas and implement them in writing. That is generally creative writing. You have to prepare for a system, because to me a game is a system of rules and outcomes, right? Successes and failures, so writing needs to be writing that is implemented into a system.

According to Robert, understanding and fully accepting the game writer's role is necessary for meeting the demands of the role and achieving personal creative fulfillment.

Like his description of understanding the mechanics of a game, Robert referred to working within the studio as understanding a system. He directly related the need for flexibility in iteration to understanding the system of production, advising:

> You need to be able to kind of sometimes turn on a dime, because if the gameplay system changes, the story changes, and what would've been the most brilliantly timed and paced story that was in your head, and was written, suddenly is no longer good simply because of the way the mechanical system changed, or the way the design changed. You have to adapt to that like immediately, or the story will not be good.

Rather than presenting this flexibility as the ability to tolerate or deal with changes, Robert indicated that owning the ever-changing process is key to making meaningful creative contributions. In this view, the game writer's craft is not bound by limitations and directives related to completing the task at hand; the game writer's craft is mastering the ability to foresee and quickly embrace changes to help the game tell the story the player will experience.

Tool proficiency. Self-teaching the basics of the skills and tools central to the other subdisciplines gives a game writer access to the lexicon of that team or group in the studio. Robert suggested an example of teaching oneself the basics of a programming language used in the game to understand the programming team's work, saying:

> I think that's good because then you get to understand how the creativity and the numbers come together. Still, I think people need to understand how logical systems work. It's almost like I wouldn't even say that someone needs to understand how programming works because language is just syntax.

Gaining knowledge about the required tools is useful in most professions, but Robert stressed how uniquely important this is for game writing. While it would be possible to simply wait for tasks to be assigned and write them to spec, understanding the tools and the thinking employed by other teams in the studio allows game writers to communicate their ideas, ultimately leading to greater creative input.

Understanding play. Robert discussed pen and paper games as tools to understand the basics of play. He noted that many game writers come out of the tabletop RPG community; this community began teaching them the skills necessary for achieving success as game writers. Even though playing tabletop games does not require the digital tools of video game development, he said, they still require the writer to create an interactive experience. Though Robert did not have a great deal of experience playing these games himself, he recognized the trend within the community and understood their potential value for game writers.

When Robert decided to seek employment in the game industry, he knew he needed to demonstrate his own understanding of play. Already a skilled writer, his next step was to apply his existing narrative skills in an interactive format. He recalled:

> I was like, "Hey, I need to make a game," so I spent a weekend with a friend who made audio. My wife did voice, and we created some interesting visual assets. It [didn't] look like a good game, but it showcased my writing. I wrote it in a little cat speak, so it showed that I could take a type of language and style and adapt it and make a game out of it. You play as a cat, and it's funny and hilarious.

Robert related this experience to demonstrate an understanding of play as a key difference between creative writers and game writers. His simple game, he felt, led to potential employers saying, "Wow, this person is serious. They spent time. They learned the tools. They figured out how to get other people behind them and make something." Robert's example demonstrated that even a simple game without expensive art and fully functioning gameplay could showcase writing.

Robert's associated learning experiences. Robert described his time in college as "a traditional liberal arts" experience. When he entered college, Robert truly believed that studying several subjects and trying many things would eventually lead to an "organic professional space." He found that traditional liberal arts, such as philosophy, psychology, and history, built his critical thinking and analysis skills. In Robert's opinion, those same courses and skills are an immensely valuable resource for writers.

Robert did concede that he was "sort of left-brained by nature," even mentioning that he entered college on a scholarship in an STEM field. While he did not pursue that course of study, he felt that left-brained thinking might be an important part of what makes a game writer stand apart from other creative writers. This might address his view of game writing as the point where creativity and the numbers come together, as well as addressing the importance he placed on systematic thinking.

Later in the conversation, Robert interjected another learning experience: a student wage job as a transcriptionist in the psychology department. He recalled taking the position to earn extra money. Though Robert had not considered the value of that experience before our interview, he decided that it helped him hone his basic skills in writing dialogue and understanding voice. Instead of composing new material, the transcriptionist must be accurate and timely. Writing requires attuning oneself to voice to practice dialogue, but more than just observing everyday speech, transcription requires thinking about words and text within a larger system.

Even though he never took a course involving writing for interactive media, Robert advised that the mastery of storytelling principles is vital for any aspiring game writer. Robert also highlighted the value of creative writing workshops beyond simply developing skills in storytelling. In his view, writing workshop experiences provide room for failure and developing the emotional maturity and flexibility a successful game writer requires.

I asked Robert if he felt that the benefits of a writing workshop could be attained on one's own. He said that, in most cases, the important skills of giving and receiving critique could not be developed in a vacuum. Game writers work with seemingly little creative control, in a chaotic environment that absolutely requires effective collaboration. In Robert's view, learning to negotiate the personalities and emotions that surface in writing workshops requires face-to-face interaction.

Robert shared that cold reading is vital in learning to deal with criticism, saying, "You had to just listen, and it was painful. Painful, but it forced me to sort of like, step back and listen." Robert also explained the value of workshop critiques:

> You have to learn to sort through: what is the good and what is the bad? Right? There in real time, or as you go off and reflect. That is the hardest thing to learn, one of the hardest things to learn in writing is when to take a note and go with it, or when to ignore a note, because you know it's not right, and to separate yourself out from that.

This learning experience correlated with Robert's work in games; he noted the importance of judgment in collaboration. Revision, he said, should not necessarily be a synthesis of all feedback received. This view was also expressed in other interviews. The giving, receiving, and judging feedback are skills that, over time, lead to better self-assessment.

Thoughts of note. Robert indicated that formal education in the technological elements of game development would have eased his transition into the game industry, but also said he would not have traded any of his learning experiences for that training. I suggested that his background in the liberal arts might have led him to even greater success. He was not convinced, saying:

> That's a tough one, because I mean… yes and no, in the sense that it gave me the talent and the skill to do what I do. It's also a series of lucky incidents and drive that got me to being paid for it.

Robert insisted that there is no golden path to game writing, or at least there has not been one in the past. His path of learning a lot, thinking a lot, writing a lot, and then making a web-based game with a talking cat was unique to him, and might not work for others.

Conclusion. Beyond the importance of the higher-order thinking skills learned through creative writing workshops, Robert mentioned the need for left-brained thinking and systems thinking in game writers. This systematic approach to game writing makes it more akin to problem-solving than composing creative work on one's own (Heussner et al., 2015). His views on education echoed Ashton's (2010) findings in two ways: first, in his view, that a liberal arts education served as valuable training for his roles in the game industry; and second that he saw the necessity for self-teaching to learn the tools and languages of other subdisciplines. Framed in terms of developing pedagogy and curriculum design, Robert's responses highlighted the value of the flexibility afforded to new CGD programs and courses. While a comprehensive approach that attempts to train students in all subdisciplines of game development may seem ideal, an approach that provides a basic understanding of those subdisciplines still equips students to succeed in the industry.

'Summary of Results

The findings from these seven interviews provide valuable insights into the lives, experiences, and work of game writers. Though no set path to a successful career as a game writer exists, and the experiences these writers shared differed significantly, core patterns regarding the essential roles of game writers and some associated areas of competence emerged. Taken in sum, these themes illuminate the phenomenon of game writing. It stands to reason, though, that a more useful analysis should consider the differences between the participants' experiences in the context of production. Doing so will allow for a clearer picture of the functional competencies required of game writers and provide a base for more effective pedagogy in CGD.

> Leveraging these shared experiences in CGD education is the next phase of this research. The following chapter [of the dissertation] discusses the significance of these findings, along with suggestions regarding how they might be applied to game writing pedagogy.
>
> And there you have it. Years of coursework and hundreds of hours spent collecting and processing data, delivered in under 40 pages. Looking back now, I appreciate that I learned far more from the process of conducting the study and working with the interview records/transcripts than I could ever put in the thesis— certainly not in a form my committee would find acceptable.
>
> This is kind of the point. As an instructor seeking to make my teaching more impactful, I was able devise new approaches to teaching game writing along the way. Another teacher might

listen to all those same interviews and come away with something different—and I see that as a positive. Even for CGD faculty who enter academe with a wealth of previous professional experience, taking on the role of educator-researcher has a positive yield no matter what.

I hope my appreciation for, and admiration of, the game writers in this study is abundantly clear. While it was tempting for the purposes of this book to reach out and seek permission to attribute these interviews, I chose to honor their original context. Ensuring anonymity allowed for the unfiltered honesty required for this study. The thing is: most of the folks you heard from in this chapter—and dozens of others that I chose to leave out of the final data set—are likely willing to share even more.

Years ago, I opened a conference talk with the rhetorical question, "Are the writers likely to have more emotional intelligence than others involved in making a game? More sensitivity? Greater perception?" A room full of game writers responded with silent glances, indicating a response of: "No, not necessarily." That humility and self-awareness is a common trait in successful game writers, whether they admit or not.

References

Ashton, D. (2010). Productive passions and everyday pedagogies: Exploring the industry-ready agenda in higher education. *Art, Design & Communication in Higher Education, 9*(1), 41–56. https://doi.org/10.1386/adch.9.1.41_1

Bates, B. (2004). *Game Design: Vol* (2nd ed.). Course PTR. http://search.ebscohost.com/login.aspx?direct=true&db=nlebk&AN=124561&site=bsi-live

Bazerman, C., & Prior, P. A. (2004). *What Writing Does and How It Does It: An Introduction to Analyzing Texts and Textual Practices*. Routledge. http://search.ebscohost.com/login.aspx?direct=true&db=nlebk&AN=102221&site=bsi-live

Campbell, J. (1972). *The Hero with a Thousand Faces* (2nd ed.). Princeton University Press.

DeMarle, M. (2007). Nonlinear game narrative. In C. M. Bateman (Ed.), *Game Writing: Narrative Skills for Videogames* (pp. 71–84). Cengage Learning.

DeVoss, D. N., Eidman-Aadahl, E., & Hicks, T. (2010). *Because Digital Writing Matters: Improving Student Writing in Online and Multimedia Environments*. Jossey-Bass.

Engeström, Y. (1999). Communication, discourse and activity. *The Communication Review, 3*(1–2), 165–185. https://doi.org/10.1080/10714429909368577

Sometimes my questions would be explicit but simple: "Should I be teaching them spec screenplays or shooting scripts?" The answers were not simple. The answers came in the conversation that followed. Rather than a debate between options, the scene played out as "Yes, and...." Instead of deciding on the best genre to emulate in class, I left the experience with a longer list of possibilities.

This was how the development of my pedagogy began. It was a real pleasure, actually: no best practices to adopt, no current research to continually follow. I was able to learn from a range of people in the field and then take that, in some form, straight into the classroom. Had I not collected data in a traditional sense in the pursuit of a doctoral thesis, my students would have still benefitted. In fact, I would not have predicted writing this book at that time.

CGD: "What to teach?" vs. "How to teach it?"

Earlier in this book, I commented on the disparate approaches to CGD in higher education—see Table 1.1 or read the full HEVGA report (Higher Education Video Game Alliance, 2015). The skilled faculty and diligent students in these programs, regardless of the program's discipline of origin, are working hard and doing really interesting things. It should be noted that not all programs are focused on AAA industry placement. The opportunities for those with game design skills continue to grow in sectors outside of entertainment.

For those programs that do focus on preparing students for the AAA space, questions of curriculum design loom large. The game industry continues to evolve; its trends shift to meet market demands incorporate advanced technology. Defining effectiveness for a curriculum by the degree to which it resembles the current industry is misguided, particularly given the bureaucratic inertia that often hinders change in higher education. Rather than focus on lists of software and techniques, CGD programs may be better served to reconsider their approach to instruction.

My research journey began in search of an answer to "What should we be teaching CGD students?" I soon realized that the answers to that question may not yield anything useful. Flashing back to the "just teach them a little screenwriting and Hero's Journey stuff" experience, I realized that my early experiences as a faculty member in CGD were likely similar to others.

Today there are hundreds of CGD programs—majors, minors, certificates, etc.—in higher education, but it appears that the pedagogy is still based on our collective best guess. This is not to say that the education students receive is not useful, or that the faculty are not engaged in improving teaching and learning.

Rather than focusing on curricular and course content, perhaps CGD would benefit from a focus on delivery. Instead of debating and determining what software and what concepts to teach, maybe we should shift energies to "How do we teach it?" Regardless of content, we know that certain habits of mind and higher order thinking skills are key to student success. Instead of analyzing industry trends in hopes of hitting that moving target, we should take a step back and think of what's at the core—the people making the games.

Those Who Can Teach...

Driven perhaps by the focus on post-graduation outcomes in higher education, an assumption that those with professional experience are best qualified to teach this content, rather than traditional academics, warrants consideration. Given the complexities of the higher education ecosystem and a game design industry that has no real uniformity in practices and processes, the resulting pedagogy would at best be a master-apprentice model; at worst, it would mean ineffective instructors who simply dazzle students with tales of industry. This is not to say that those transitioning from the game industry to academia cannot be successful; rather, it means that those individuals succeed because of their willingness and agility in synthesizing professional experience with best practices.

Passion for the medium, empathy for and belief in students' abilities, and skill in mentoring amplify previous experience. Implicit in the cliché "those who can't, teach" is an assumption that "those who can (or did), can teach." Regardless of your preference for cliché or assumption, or the background of the instructor, beyond questions of course content and teaching practice is an even more intriguing two-part question—why do we teach it this way; how do we know if it's working?

Collectively, we already know a great deal about teaching and learning, about human development. Scholars and researchers from a range of disciplines have continued to grow the corpus of literature regarding teaching and learning in their subjects. Still laying the foundations of a new field of study, CGD faculty would be well-served to seek out this knowledge. The synthesis of personal experience, professional experience, and relevant scholarship will reveal pathways to effective pedagogy in the field.

Reflecting on past experience to reveal and make use of tacit knowledge is only the first step. Relying on those with expertise in teaching, learning from what they have learned, gives reflection a concrete objective. Rather than just sharing stories "from the trenches" to give credence to their teaching methods—hoping students think, "Wow, they must really know what they're talking about"—instructors would be better served to situate their prior experience in appropriate conceptual frameworks laid out by educational researchers.

Bridging Education and Industry through Scholarship

My initial intention was to better understand the game industry and its relationship to CGD in higher education. Early efforts that I now call a pilot study did not seem promising in the wide range of experiences and opinions I came across. One major issue that arose in a number of interviews was participants' willingness, eagerness even, to tell me how we should fix CGD. It was clear that these individuals had an axe to grind; it seemed to me that their problem was more philosophical, an issue with higher education and its relationship to industry generally.

Flash forward a few months. After processing the pilot study, I knew sharper focus was necessary for a successful study. The decision to examine game writers, specifically, was suggested to me by a colleague in Composition Studies. She pointed out that despite my fascination with uncovering tacit knowledge, I had neglected to factor in my own years of experience in the classroom—my "expertise" could be the key to processing and making use of the data collected from practitioners in the field.

This was the moment I embraced the role of educator-researcher. In my head, it was now clear:

> Their job is to write for games. My job is to teach. Rather than ask them how or what I should teach, I should focus how and what they do as game writers. Then it is up to me to make sense of that and apply it to teaching.

As CGD seeks to collaborate with industry, this distinction of roles gets muddy. Input from industry is vital but only insofar as programs are able to operationalize it in the classroom.

Realizing that I was the key to this fusion of professionals' experience and sound pedagogy was a breakthrough. Situating myself as a partner in the co-creation of knowledge, rather than an outsider trying to record the experiences of others, finally brought my research design to life. The next step was ensuring that my study was part of larger, ongoing conversations in higher education.

Returning to the "academic, theoretical stuff" opened doors for my work. Identifying relevant lines of inquiry, research methods, and pedagogical frameworks from established disciplines brought clarity. My impulse was to learn more from game writers in the field—speak with more writers, spend time observing, etc. That would have meant more data, but still no way forward to my ultimate goal of improving pedagogy. The way forward was learning from the thinkers, researchers, and educators that came before in order to operationalize my findings as enhanced, research-informed instruction.

The relative novelty of video games as a medium makes it tempting to eschew the conventions of higher education and disciplinary traditions. CGD educators are teaching something that has not been taught before, preparing students to create in a medium on the cutting edge of entertainment and technology. The foundations of teaching and learning remain valuable and failing to incorporate them into our pursuit of CGD education is folly. Embracing theories and research from relevant fields broadens the opportunity for more innovation in teaching CGD. We can nurture more innovative designers who will, in time, lead to a more innovative industry and medium.

Fusing the Languages of Industry and Education

According to Daniel Ashton (2010), "[c]ollaboration, dialogue and attempts to bridge industry and higher education gaps seem to be focused primarily on workforce development" (p. 44), resulting in tensions between the programs and the industry. Educational programs seek to enrich students, leading to innovation in the medium (i.e., better games). The industry is focused on profit-driven motives (i.e., a better industry). Obviously, a balance between the two is necessary. A decade since Ashton's observations, the tension still exists.

Rather than looking to the industry for what specific, imminently obsolete, tools to teach CGD programs would better serve students through a focus on student development more broadly. Transferable skills in communication, collaboration, and critical thinking enhance students' employability, generally, across industries. In a complex development process like AAA game development, these skills seem even more important. These are skills we know how to teach—or at least have access to established approaches—in higher education.

A mathematical aside: A typical three-credit course in 15-week semester meets 150 minutes per week or there abouts. Minus assigned work outside of class meetings, that equals 37.5 hours of instruction. There's some irony here: 37.5 hours resembles a 40-hour work week, but it also falls just short of that number. Depending on your point of view, this could mean different things. It might reveal the difficulty of course design and the skill of instructors who are effective; conversely, a cynic cites the 2.5-hour deficit as evidence that education cannot prepare students for "the real world." It's a figure many find surprising; they probably never thought about it before. I just like pointing it out at cocktail parties—and books, apparently.

Graduates strong in higher order thinking skills, with the flexibility and ability to learn new tools and adapt to different contexts, are what the industry needs. With some baseline competency in their game development discipline of choice, regardless of the particular game engine or modeling software used in their coursework, they will get up to speed with greater ease and contribute to the studio's efforts quickly. More importantly, these well-developed graduates will have an enhanced capacity for innovation and creativity—in any field they might choose post-graduation.

The approach of this study allows instructors and scholars to leverage the practical realities of the industry to enhance instruction. It can be difficult to develop pedagogies in creative fields, but, as Mayers (2005) suggests, engaging existing frameworks to theorize practice can help fields learn from each other. Emerging CGD programs looking to enhance pedagogy could engage practitioners to explore the factors that inform their work in context. There is little uniformity across the industry and limited access is granted to researchers, but skilled educator-researchers can leverage the lived experiences of practitioners to inform course design and instruction.

References

Ashton, D. (2010). Productive passions and everyday pedagogies: Exploring the industry-ready agenda in higher education. *Art, Design & Communication in Higher Education, 9*(1), 41–56. https://doi.org/10.1386/adch.9.1.41_1

Higher Education Video Game Alliance. (2015). *Our State of Play: Higher Education Video Game Alliance Survey 2014–2015.* http://glsstudios.com/hevga/wp-content/themes/hevga_theme/assets/2015_HEVGA_Survey_Results.pdf

Mayers, T. (2005). *(Re)Writing Craft: Composition, Creative Writing, and the Future of English Studies.* University of Pittsburgh Press.

5 Areas of Competence, Essential Roles

If one looks past the basic trappings of higher education—syllabi, exams, grades, course scheduling, etc.—they will see that uniformity from course to course, instructor to instructor is hard to find. We speak the same language but have different things to say and different ways to say it. Rather than offering, "Here is the optimal way to teach game writing based on my research and scholarship..." I sought to create space in my findings through my 3×5 framework for game writing pedagogy, space for myself and others to craft effective pedagogy.

Spending time with the data from my study did not reveal an explicit definition of professional game writing—game writing is not one thing, not even two or three or four, but different tasks all at once at different times. Rather than identifying finite abilities, skills, and knowledge, this study revealed the areas of competence necessary for game writing, including:

- writing and storytelling,
- communication and collaboration,
- understanding systems and dynamics,
- tool proficiency, and
- understanding play.

In addition to these areas of competence, the study identified three essential roles of the game writer—wordsmith, sensemaker, and advocate—that serve as a structure for examining how various areas of competence are engaged, alone or in combination, across the array of tasks performed by industry game writers.

Essential Roles

Considering some essential roles of the game writer may provide valuable insight for CGD programs and the game industry. Common

DOI: 10.4324/9781003277668-5

misconceptions about game writing and the role of the game writer in context are considered some of the reasons storytelling in games has suffered in the past (Dansky, 2007). Similarly, instructors who conceive of game writing as a mere collection of written works commonly created in the industry are not likely to produce anything more than a list of possible classroom activities. Incorporating coursework that resembles the game writing in terms of rhetorical genre (i.e., the process in context), preferably in a face-to-face environment, is valuable.

Instructors who frame pedagogy with these essential roles offer students a sense of the changing contexts in which they will produce work. If challenged to do so, students can conceive of any given task in terms of hypothetical industry contexts—the rhetorical situation and its situation within the activity system—while relating them to a combination of these essential roles. Rather than learning to do one thing well, students will develop a capacity to taking on an array of associated tasks.

Example: Students can be tasked to create a dialogue sequence for a game. Starting from scratch as wordsmiths, they must analyze the affordances and constraints of the platform to shape their words—"What's the word count?" "What information do we have about the characters?" "Will this be voiced?" If asked to add dialogue to an existing game, they become sensemakers providing context for the player's actions—"What led us to this point?" "How does the player beat this level?" If they are working as writers on a larger, collaborative studio project, they must become advocates to ensure the quality of the game's story is upheld by effectively communicating with other members of the team—"How much time will it take to change that artwork? Is it worth it?" "Does this scene really add anything to the story?" The writer is working toward the same goal in all three roles, but must prioritize differently depending on their role at that given time.

Areas of Competence for Game Writers

This exploration of game writing practices sheds new light on the process; however, fitting the work of the game writer into neat categories proved difficult. The areas of competence—writing and storytelling, communication and collaboration, understanding systems and dynamics, tool proficiency, and understanding play—were employed as organizational tools in this study. The roles and functions associated with these areas of competence overlap in significant ways, depending on the setting and the project involved. Identifying these areas of competence and their relation to one another, in addition to points of intersection with other subdisciplines in game development, creates a space for designing effective courses and curricula in CGD that incorporate the vital component of storytelling in games.

Writing and Storytelling

The two most important patterns that emerged within this area of competence were the game writer's need to create engaging narrative material and do so with efficiency and flexibility. Henry stated bluntly, for instance, "Obviously, you need to be able to tell a good story." Micah and Robert extended the sentiment by noting that game writers must tell good stories within any given constraints of format or time. Across the interviews, the list of required elements for success in game writing included writing concisely, understanding story structure, writing evocative dialogue, understanding and adopting voice, developing characters, and grasping the basic mechanics of writing. Given that this area of competence is likely relevant to all narrative writing, it is notable that interviewees often presented these elements as obvious requirements and focused instead on the differences between game writing and other creative writing fields.

Communication and Collaboration

Though valuable in any profession, well-developed communication and collaboration skills are essential to the game writer's role in production. Those writers who develop additional skills in design and leadership have the potential to elevate their value to an organization. Learning the lexicons of the other subdiscipline teams involved in production affords clarity that allows the game writer greater creative input.

As one's skills evolve, they can approach an understanding of the creative visions of others. Lou and Garreth indicated the importance of coupling communication and collaboration with emotional intelligence, which allows the game writer to develop a sense of what is important to collaborators across subdisciplines, ultimately helping others feel ownership in the telling of the game's story.

Understanding Systems and Dynamics

In the context of game development, game writers must understand the systems and dynamics of both the game and the game's production. Beyond a basic understanding of interactivity and play, the game writer must understand how the player will engage with and experience the game. Peter offered the example of writing in conjunction with the game's platform, referencing the different affordances and restrictions of creating stories through on-screen text bubbles in a mobile game versus voice-acted dialogue in a more robust AAA title.

Game writers must also understand the underlying structures and hierarchy of both the creative decision-making and the roles of the other subdisciplines in the studio. Rather than the ability to merely choose one's battles, mastering these systems allows the game writer to maximize their creative input and productivity. Robert framed this area of competence as knowing how to navigate his day, referring to the many meetings and other office functions that might pull him away from the tasks at hand. Garreth added some depth from a leadership perspective, explaining how narrative-focused creative choices have consequences for those on other subdiscipline teams. Understanding the system of production allowed him to make more effective creative decisions.

Tool Proficiency

The participants noted the increasing need for aspiring game writers to use, or at least have a firm understanding of, industry-relevant tools. Tool proficiency allows aspiring game writers to demonstrate their understanding of interactivity and, in some cases, allows for clearer communication of their ideas to designers. In Henry's case, his ability to teach himself tools allowed him to execute some of his own ideas in game-specific software that made those ideas clearer to designers, thus increasing the odds of implementation.

The ability to manipulate conceptual and technological tools is also vital given the many forms the text of game writing can take. Peter emphasized the need for tool manipulation in his discussion of spreadsheets, mentioning how writers must solve problems regarding organization and tracking information. Given the varying needs of projects, and the frequency of unexpected changes outside the control of the game writer, this ability to manipulate tools is vital to success.

Understanding Play

Understanding play is the key difference between writing in other mediums and game writing. In their interviews, the participants mentioned that skilled writers from other mediums who do not understand play usually fail in their attempts to transition into the game industry. Margaret's statement about letting players interact with the world how they choose to, even if that is not what she might prefer herself, is an example of this. The game writer must anticipate, and honor, the player's wishes.

Understanding play is also a necessary part of game writers accepting their roles, and sometimes limited creative control, during the development process. As Garreth shared, if a game writer is sacrificing the game's playability to tell the game's story, they are in the wrong business. A grasp of the player's interactive experience allows the game writer to anticipate the potential actions of the player.

Thoughts of Note

Due to the necessary collaboration between game writers, other subdisciplines (e.g., art, audio, programming), and player expectations of interactivity, these areas of competence represent the differences between writing for games and writing in other mediums. The specific framing of these areas of competence by the interviewees is also noteworthy, as their responses directed to both students and professional writers in other mediums were similar in many ways. In both cases, a strong foundation in creative writing and storytelling is assumed as a prerequisite for employment. Regardless of the specific areas of competence discussed, the responses were generally focused on debunking the perceived myths about a writer's work in preparation for the practical realities of the field.

Reference

Dansky, R. (2007). Introduction to game narrative. In C. M. Bateman (Ed.), *Game Writing: Narrative Skills for Videogames* (pp. 1–23). Cengage Learning.

Approaching Flexibility

As game writers do not often control the direction the game's story will take, they must adapt to different scenarios and be prepared to respond to changes throughout development. Writers require this flexibility, as they must recognize multiple audiences: the writing team, the person or group requesting the changes, and, ultimately, the player. Incorporating these elements in the classroom requires creativity and a playful environment. One example of this approach is destabilizing authorship in revision. Though it could take several forms, the basic concept involves tasking students with the completion of work initiated by others. As a result, students practice flexibility in the execution of peer-initiated work while taking steps to promote clarity in their own writing in hopes of communicating their original vision to peer collaborators.

Incorporating time-sensitive writing in class simulates the studio experience; provides a look into the practices of the game writer; and challenges students' creativity, flexibility, and efficiency. Complicating these exercises with intermittent changes in direction, further restrictions to format, or additional content demands that students practice an iterative approach to game writing practice. Timed exercises to achieve this goal can be as simple as demanding changes in length or limiting student word choice (i.e., "You may not repeat any words in this 100-word story," or "You are forbidden from using monosyllabic words in this scene.") once the activity is underway. Asking students to engage in these activities in a safe, perhaps comical, environment exposes them to the practice of game writing they will experience in the workplace.

Requiring students to work as teams may lessen the potential stress of these situations for students with learning disabilities or physical limitations that make time-sensitive exercises daunting. For all students, making these activities low stakes in terms of graded assessment serves to lessen creative anxiety and promote productive failure. Students can be taught to appreciate the value of Micah's sentiment, "We don't have time to do it right the first time, but we have time to do it five or six times."

As an instructor, the hypothetical possibilities for simulating fast-paced, hectic industry scenarios in the classroom are many, although the traditional, semester-based structure of coursework in American higher education can present a challenge in replicating what game writers encounter in the studio environment. Students meet face-to-face with instructors for roughly 37.5 hours per week, ironically close to the standard industry work week. A course model that replicates a standard industry work week is worth exploring, but other alternatives can present similar benefits.

Emulating day-long game writing-intensive workshops, such as those at the Game Developers Conference and East Coast Game Conference, in course design is difficult due to administrative hurdles, but exploring their potential in the form of extracurricular activity circumvents scheduling challenges and course structure restrictions. If presented as non-credit or non-graded opportunities, extracurricular options also provide an environment for productive failure with the added benefit of welcoming interested students outside of CGD programs. This allows students to expand their network of peer collaborators to include students from other academic programs and possibly those in the community outside the university.

The final hurdle to incorporating flexibility is assessment. Deciding how to measure the degree to which a student has improved or achieved mastery in this area presents an opportunity for CGD programs to challenge traditional notions of assessment. With no established scale to consult in flexibility-related learning outcomes, levels of competence and means of demonstrating outcomes are open to determination.

Approaching Tools

Understanding the tools, both conceptual and technical, and skills of other game subdisciplines gives the game writer access to the lexicon of that team or group in the studio. Helping students gain familiarity with tools is common across CGD curricula. Access to these tools and instruction in their use provide aspiring game writers with a unique advantage over writers in other fields. It stands to reason that tool proficiency is best demonstrated through creating playable demos to show employers; however, giving students a foundation that allows them to manipulate tools of any kind has intrinsic value that will enhance their future work.

Pen-and-paper games are an excellent way to teach interactivity and provide writers with the opportunity to work with a set of conceptual tools. Student-written pen-and-paper games that feature different combat systems, character attributes, and rule sets demand clarity in both conception and execution. Incorporating revision into these kinds of writing assignments increases their value. An iterative approach to developing these projects, whether for one's own game of that of a peer, requires students to consider writing fundamentals and design aspects in parallel. Similar revisions to narrative design can work in much the same way, highlighting the sensemaking required to add context to a set of preexisting rules and mechanics or to incorporate others' ideas for changes into the narrative.

Effective game writing courses incorporate tools other than word processors to practice writing. Asking students to write with spreadsheets, for example, challenges students to think of their written work as more than a linear narrative or words on a page. It allows them to design and implement delivery systems for branching narratives in a space larger than a standard sheet of paper or to test the balance of character attributes by utilizing the formula and function features, rather than simply recording and refining concepts through text. Students must make decisions regarding how they will present information to both the player and the other members of the development team by situating their contribution as a component of the larger production and eventual product. Coupled with discussion and analysis of their design choices, pushing students in this direction requires them to think in terms of tool manipulation.

Encouraging students to think critically about the existing tools of the trade is also important. The user communities of game development tools commonly create and share tools, such as *Fungus* for Unity 3D or *Screenwriter* for Unreal Engine, for incorporating dialogue into games. Requiring students to research and discuss these add-ons provides a chance to offer critique in terms of trends and perceived needs in the game development community.

Note: Faculty should avoid evangelizing the primacy of any particular software, as it may limit students' capacity for self-teaching any of the tools they may face in a professional setting. We may have our favorites and strongly held opinions for a particular tool's superiority, but we should not be teachers of software—the internet can do that. If one frames instruction that's based on concepts applicable across platforms, exchanging depth for breadth is a greater benefit to students.

Students may fail to see the relevance of this work, as it does not result in a working game demo for their portfolio. This study, however, reveals that a major challenge for aspiring game writers is a failure to understand, or demonstrate understanding of, interactivity and the tools associated with it. CGD students have ample opportunities to learn the digital tools of the trade. HEVGA's 2015 survey of programs found that coursework in programming, animation, art, audio, and other digital tools was offered or required at most schools (Higher Education Video Game Alliance, 2015). Aspiring game writers studying CGD can apply what they learn in these courses to demonstrate both their knowledge of game development processes and their deep understanding of interactivity.

Approaching Storytelling

The demands placed on game writers can be met only when the storytelling fundamentals are in place; consequently, covering these principles is crucial. Given the limited number of game-narrative-focused courses offered across CGD programs, though, game writing courses must prioritize what content to include. Where it is not practical to cover all the necessary competencies in the few CGD courses offered, looking to other disciplines is a practical approach.

Any course that requires reading, analysis, and writing offers a chance to build the skills of the game writer. CGD programs can work with college requirements and collaborate with other departments to shape curricular options that strengthen students' abilities in game writing. Courses in mythology, fiction, film, and drama may fulfill university general education requirements for students while also providing them with the knowledge of storytelling fundamentals so important to game writing. Encouraging students to explore works outside of the Western canon also prepares them to innovate in the medium by challenging the conventional narratives found in games. Analyzing the way stories are told in games is vital, but it is also important that students be encouraged to engage with literature, film, and other media and texts outside of standard video game fare to focus on how stories work and how characters are developed. CGD programs can promote this mindset in coursework and curriculum design by adding a requirement that expands students' knowledge of storytelling and play in other cultures.

Another vital component of teaching game writing is the incorporation of traditional writing workshop elements. This study highlights the value of the workshop experience beyond providing opportunities to practice writing. The participants framed these learning experiences as places to develop emotional intelligence and skills in giving, receiving, and assessing feedback. Specifically, the interviewees assigned great value to the "cold read" experiences that require writers to deliver work to the class and observe others reading it aloud.

Traditional workshop components can also be incorporated into game writing coursework. Some of the forms game writing takes may not be conducive to cold readings: sitting in a circle to read a list of 100 variations of "argh, you shot me" or a hypothetical community blog post may not provide the same emotional stakes as reading other

Conclusion

Effective instructors possess great power, the kind that comes with great responsibility. Regardless of the specific course content or delivery mode, engaging students and challenging them to (really) think, (actually) make, and (successfully) communicate has a lasting impact. Many of these powerful instructors have been teaching game narrative/writing and other game design disciplines for decades, and successfully; the aforementioned "best practices" continue to develop under their stewardship.

The approaches outlined above might be your current teaching practices, or they may seem completely foreign. I encourage you to try something new. See how you might adopt one of these practices and mold it to suit your purpose. It could be as simple as how you frame things for your students. Make the value of their work explicit. Communicate that what they do in your class is just one small piece of what they will need to be successful; that the semester-long course is just a pathway to more learning.

Active, curious, dedicated educators know there is always more to learn—or, at the very least, some else to learn. Testing out new approaches to pedagogy keeps things interesting for you and fresh for your students. In any discipline, there are no right or wrong ways to teach, but there are certainly good and bad ways to go about it. Remaining open to learning from others in order to improve and evolve pedagogy is a good way to move forward.

Reference

Higher Education Video Game Alliance. (2015). Our state of play: Higher education video game alliance survey 2014–2015. http://glsstudios.com/hevga/wp-content/themes/hevga_theme/assets/2015_HEVGA_Survey_Results.pdf

Epilogue

The greatest stories—most poignant, culturally impactful, memorable—of this century will be told in videogames. Enthusiasts who celebrate games' primacy in this arena are mistaken, blinded by the allure of technological novelty. The truth: games have only begun to reveal their potential to players. Devotees cite interactivity and immersion as qualities unique to the medium, but these claims do not hold up to scrutiny. Novels transport readers to new worlds and travelers lose themselves via tiny back-of-seat airline screens when the stories are wrought with care and attention to the audience.

From a cynic's point of view, interactivity and immersion are just fancy words to say "I love games and think they're better than other stuff." A hundred years from now, give or take, what we will say about games' ability to tell stories once the medium matures? Only the transformation from technology to entertainment, entertainment to art, will reveal the true value of games.

That's I hope to situate myself now. Heeding Donald Norman's (1999) claim that "[t]he value of any technology lies in the pedagogy that informs it." The computer game design (CGD) educators in higher education, of which I count myself a member, pursue the medium with passion, looking to advance "beyond computer science and art to simply code games and make them look good" (Salmond, 2016). This book represents a step in that direction, a bridge between higher education and game industry practice.

Admittedly, this bridge is more the dubious ropes connecting rickety old boards type, that ultimately breaks but our protagonist is someone able to hold on and avoid falling into the chasm variety, than your Sydney Harbour or Golden Gate kind. Combining methods from Writing Studies and best practices in higher education, I sought a pedagogy of game writing that leveraged the experiences of practitioners in the field. Across levels of experience—both within the industry and with their

Other participants in my study highlighted the differences between "doing the work" and "getting paid to do it." This sentiment acknowledges that although one may possess the skills and abilities necessary for performing the tasks of the game writer, starting out and ultimately succeeding in the industry requires more than just the relevant skills. There is some luck involved; there is also requisite diligence and professionalism.

For CGD educators, this is a reminder that any education that provides students with challenges, demands rigor, fosters community, and values communication is the first step toward success post-graduation. Teaching students the requisite skills to make games is obviously important, but the failing to develop students beyond technical expertise does them a disservice.

Finding Fulfillment

Reflecting on my research—really, trying to drill down on this "doing" vs. "getting paid to do it" sentiment—I found a framework that might guide our efforts in curriculum development. I suggest the following:

- Preparing students to find industry employment requires basic knowledge of the game development process and current trends in the field.
- Preparing students to do the work once employed requires understanding industry roles and their daily functions.
- Preparing students to succeed and innovate in the field requires practicing the competencies necessary for performing these roles across contexts, analyzing industry trends in content and practices, and possessing the flexibility and emotional intelligence to work well with others.

I sought to test this framework in an off-the-record conversation with an industry veteran years after my dissertation—still seeking to learn from the experience of others, still wanting some assurance that my findings would ultimately assist students.

With a slow nod and eventual smile, the veteran game designer supported this framework but suggested it might be stated more simply: "Yea, sure. Basically, instead of just helping them get hired, you want to help them have satisfying careers." That is it. Perhaps after two decades in higher education, more indoctrinated in the prevailing culture than I realize, I failed to see that real objective of my work (and the work I am encouraging others to do).

My study began with a desire to teach game writing "the right way." One 15-week course and just 37.5 hours of instruction: I did not want to mess up. I began with the assumption that there were best practices to be discovered and employed in my teaching. Upon reflection, aided by colleagues and friends, I was ultimately reminded giving the confidence to have agency over their academic and future careers, providing them with opportunities for creative growth and professional development, is the key.

Preparing students to find fulfillment post-graduation, no matter what career path they ultimately choose, should be our goal. Remaining agile in our thinking and receptive to both industry and colleagues from other disciplines, CGD educators can help ensure our collective achievement of this goal. Continuing to evolve my practices through research and scholarship also makes my role more fulfilling as I am certain it will for any educator who chooses to do the same. Over time, sharing the accretion of our research, scholarship, and pedagogical practices may lead to a "right way" to teach CGD; I sincerely hope it does not.

That's all for now. Thanks for reading.

References

Norman, D. A. (1999). *The Invisible Computer: Why Good Products Can Fail, the Personal Computer Is So Complex, and Information Appliances Are the Solution* (Reprint edition). The MIT Press.

Russell, D. R. (2001). Where do the naturalistic studies of WAC/WID point to. *WAC for the New Millennium: Strategies for Continuing Writing-across-Thecurriculum Programs*, 259–298. http://files.eric.ed.gov/fulltext/ED454552.pdf#page=272

Salmond, M. (2016). *Video Game Design: Principles and Practices from the Ground up*. Fairchild Books.

Index

Note: **Bold** page numbers refer to tables.

AAA game industry 3, 5–6, 12, 21, 37, 86, 89
academic disciplines 5, 25
activity theory model 21; *see also* cultural-historical activity theory (CHAT)
advocate 39, 51, 53, 55, 57, 58, 69, 91
American higher education 98
artistic expression 12, 13
Ashton, D. 82, 89
authorship 4, 46, 77, 97, 98, 102

Bateman, Chris 18

Campbell, Joseph 58
Chandler, Raphael 23
Character Development and Storytelling for Games (Sheldon) 17
cinematic cutscenes 12, 62
classroom 85, 88, 92; experimentation in 104; implementation in 96–97
classroom implementation: approaching systems 102; attitudes 97; CGD coursework 105; experimentation in 104; flexibility 98–99; interactivity 103–104; relevant coursework 104–105; specialty-specific portfolios 105; storytelling 101–102; tools 99–101
collaborative intelligence 97

comics 46, 49, 57, 69, 73
communication and collaboration 40, 42, 43, 47, 53, 58, 64, 70, 77, 89, 93
competence: areas of 91; communication and collaboration 40, 93; for game writers 92–93; tool proficiency 40, 94; understanding play 40, 95; understanding systems and dynamics 40, 94; writing and storytelling 40, 93
computer game design (CGD) 1; course availability **4**; game development 3; game writing in 16; higher education 2, 86; importance of 18; industry-grade tools 3; opportunity for 99; skilled labor 2
computer programming 2
conversation 11, 14, 26, 30, 37, 39, 41, 50, 58, 59, 80, 85, 89, 110
cooperation 97
creative activity 3, 31
creative writing 17, 20
critical reception 13–14
critical thinking 4, 44, 80, 89
cultural-historical activity theory (CHAT) 21–23, 57, 68, 108, 109
culture fit 42

Dansky, Richard 10
data collection 28–31
decision-making 54, 63

design documentation 10, 16, 18
Despain, Wendy 17
Developer's Dilemma: The Secret World of Videogame Creators (O'Donnell) 28
DeVoss, D. N. 45
DigiPen Institute of Technology 6
digital age 20
drama production 21
Dungeons and Dragons (D&D) 65
dynamics 21, 43, 48, 53, 54, 56, 59, 94, 102

education 2, 6, 10, 31, 40, 44–46, 49, 88, 109
educator-researcher context 20–26
emotional intelligence 31, 51, 53, 93, 97
employability post-graduation 85
Engeström, Y. 21, 57
Entertainment Software Association 5
enthusiasm 41, 45, 51, 62, 65, 66, 109
entry-level writers 16
essential roles 39, 91–92
ethnographic approaches 28
evidence-based pedagogy 7
Extra Credits web series 6

Facebook games 38
family resemblance approach 23
feedback 43, 44, 47, 49, 56, 81
fiction writer 19, 51, 56
Foot, K. A. 21, 57
formal education 31, 40, 44, 46, 51, 57, 61, 62, 81
formulaic models 12
Frankensteining 55
freedom 12, 16, 28, 97
freelance writer 46
functional competencies 39–40

game design document (GDD) 10
game development: complexity of 22; curriculum design 7–8; disparate disciplines 4–6; industry perceptions 6–7; knowledge of 101; technical components of 4

game industry: career path in 41; challenges researching 28; employment in 19; evolution of 12; family resemblance approach 23
Game Narrative Review competition 103
games-as-career student 3
games-enthusiast student 2
Game Studies movement 6
game writers: advocate 39; characteristics of 97; competence areas 92–93; coursework 97; functional competencies of 37; sensemaker 39; wordsmith 39
game writing: community 42, 85; conceptual framework 20; critical reception 13–14; data collection 28–31; definitions and perceptions 20, 91; educator-researcher context 20–26; functional competencies 18; game writers writing 14–16; higher education context 16–20; importance of 14; industry inertia 11–13; narrative design 15; pedagogy 102, 108; productive career in 40; role confusion 9–11; time-sensitive nature 43
Game Writing: Narrative Skills for Videogames (Bateman) 18
Garreth 62–69
GDC Vault website 103
Goldsmith, Kenneth 20
Guzdial, M. 42

Henry 69–75
The Hero with a Thousand Faces (Campbell) 58
Heussner, T. 15
Hewner, M. 42
higher education 2; basic trappings of 91; context 16–20; essential roles 91; post-graduation outcomes 87
Higher Education Video Game Association (HEVGA) 5, 86
higher learning 68
horror stories 16
human development 87

IGDA Writers SIG 103
implementation 96–97
industry inertia 11–13
innovation 12, 89
inquiry 12, 25, 89
instruction, implications for 18–19
internship 3
interrelationships 23

Jacobs, Stephen 11
Journalism 105

language 21, 38, 68, 91
learning experiences 44, 61, 67
liberal arts education 82
Lou 51–57
ludology 103

Margaret 40–45
market behavior 10
Maxwell, J. A. 25
Mayers, T. 20, 90
McAllister, K. S. 28
Micah 46–51
Microsoft Excel 60
Miles, M. B. 30
multiple audiences 42, 98

Nardi, B. A. 21
narrative design 15, 52, 71, 100, 105
narrative designer 16, 41, 42, 52, 58
Newman, J. 12
non-digital games 104
non-fiction 57
Norman, D. A. 11, 107
numerous authorities 12

objectivity 54, 55
O'Donnell, Casey 28
opportunity 45, 85
organizational structures 60
Our State of Play (2015) 5

parallel place 54
pedagogical research 31
pedagogy 24, 96, 102–103, 106–108
pen-and-paper games 99
personal experience 87
Peter 57–61
Peterson, M. 18

phenomenological research 25
phenomenology 25
physical sales 15
Portnow, James 6
post-graduation outcomes 87
pragmatic validity 26
Prior, Paul 18, 61
production system 55, 62
productive criticism 43
professional experience 37
professional game writers 36, 51, 73
profit-driven motives 89
programming language 79
project course 4
Pulp Fiction movie 50

qualitative research design 25

*The Reflective Practitioner: How
    Professionals Think in Action*
    (Schön) 23–24
rhetorical genre studies (RGS)
    22–23, 57, 75, 108
Robert 75–82
role confusion 9–11
Russell, D. R. 22

scholarship 3, 88, 91, 108
Schön, Donald 23, 57
screenwriting 17, 72, 86, 102, 104
self-assessment 51, 69, 74, 81, 102,
    104
self-teaching 57, 79, 82, 100
sensemaker 38, 39, 45, 51, 57, 75,
    91, 92
sensemaking 38, 46, 47, 49, 51, 58,
    65, 71, 100
Shakespeare 14, 73
Sheldon, Lee 17
skilled labor 2
skilled writers 11, 64, 72, 79, 95, 108
skilled writing 12
Skolnick, E. 51
sound instructional principles 7, 96
sound theoretical assumptions 26
Stoddard, Brandes 19
"Story Medics, Story Robots,
    Script Monkeys, and the Words
    Person" 15
storytelling concepts 1, 40, 41, 93

student development 89
Suckling, M. 15
Swales, John 22, 23

tacit knowledge 23–24, 45, 85
Taylor, J. R. 38
teaching game writing 82, 101, 106
technical writing 17
three-act structure 58
time-sensitive nature 43, 98
tool proficiency 40, 43, 48, 94
traditional writing 17, 101, 105
Tschang, F. T. 28

Uncreative Writing: Managing Language in the Digital Age (Goldsmith) 20
understanding play 40, 43, 49, 56, 60, 66, 72, 93, 95
understanding systems and dynamics 40, 43, 48, 59, 65, 78, 93, 94

Unity 3D 100

value empathy 97
Van Every, E. J. 38
video game industry 12
video games 11, 16; mechanics of 43; as medium makes 89
Vygotskiĭ, L. S. 21

Walton, M. 15
Wolf, Mark 11
wordsmith 39, 45, 51, 69, 71, 75, 91
wordsmithing role 41, 69
workplace environment 43
writing and storytelling 40, 41, 46, 51, 58, 62, 69, 75, 93
writing instruction 9, 10, 16, 22, 45, 58, 97, 102, 108
writing skills 10, 18, 43, 44, 49, 59
Writing Studies 1, 107
written communication 3, 10

For Product Safety Concerns and Information please contact our EU
representative GPSR@taylorandfrancis.com
Taylor & Francis Verlag GmbH, Kaufingerstraße 24, 80331 München, Germany